Kierkegaard's Philosophy of Becoming

SUNY Series in Theology and Continental Thought

Douglas L. Donkel, editor

Kierkegaard's Philosophy of Becoming

Movements and Positions

Clare Carlisle

State University of New York Press

Cover image: Kierkegaard Library, St. Olaf College.

Published by
State University of New York Press, Albany

© 2005 State University of New York

All rights reserved

Printed in the United States of America

No part of this book may be used or reproduced in any manner whatsoever
without written permission. No part of this book may be stored in a retrieval system
or transmitted in any form or by any means including electronic, electrostatic,
magnetic tape, mechanical, photocopying, recording, or otherwise
without the prior permission in writing of the publisher.

For information, address State University of New York Press, Albany, NY
www.sunypress.edu

Production by Judith Block
Marketing by Anne M. Valentine

Library of Congress Cataloging-in-Publication Data

Carlisle, Clare, 1977-
   Kierkegaard's philosophy of becoming : movements and positions /
     Clare Carlisle.
      p. cm — (SUNY series in theology and continental thought)
   Includes bibliographical references and index.
   ISBN 0-7914-6547-0 (hardcover : alk. paper) — ISBN 0-7914-6548-9
(pbk. : alk. paper)
  1. Kierkegaard, Søren, 1813-1855. I. Title. II. Series.

B377.C314 2005
198'.9—dc22

2004027566

10 9 8 7 6 5 4 3 2 1

For Jemima

I wasn't sorry to see something move, it was a change from all those motionless existences which watched me like staring eyes. I said to myself, as I followed the swaying of the branches: "Movements never quite exist, they are transitions, intermediaries between two existences, unaccented beats." I got ready to see them come out of nothingness, gradually ripen, blossom: at last I was going to surprise existences in the process of being born.

⁂ Jean-Paul Sartre, *Nausea*

Contents

Acknowledgments   xi

Introduction: The Place and the Path   1

PART ONE

   1. Metaphysics of Motion   9

   2. The Logic of Becoming   23

   3. Kierkegaard's Critique of Hegel   33

PART TWO

   4. *Either/Or*: Kierkegaard's Principle of Contradiction   49

   5. *Repetition*: The Possibility of Motion   67

   6. *Fear and Trembling*: A Higher Plane   91

PART THREE

    7. Becoming a Christian   113

    8. Beyond Philosophy?   127

    9. Repetitions   137

Notes   149

Bibliography   163

Index   171

Acknowledgments

I am grateful to Trinity College, Cambridge, and the University of Cambridge for providing the financial support and resources that enabled me to undertake the research presented here. I also wish to thank the Leverhulme Trust and the School of Theology and Religious Studies at the University of Leeds for my present Research Fellowship.

Most of all I thank George Pattison for his guidance, encouragement, and patience, and especially for offering me his time and his wisdom so graciously.

Mike Weston, Daniel Wilson, and Nigel Warburton have read and commented on the text at various stages in its development, and their advice has been invaluable. I am also indebted to Jon Stewart for allowing me to use his translations of texts by Kierkegaard's contemporaries.

A special thank you to Don Cupitt, who first taught me philosophy and theology, and who introduced me to Kierkegaard. I could not have had a more inspiring teacher. I am very grateful to Don and his wife Susan for all their kindness and generosity during the last few years.

Finally I would like to thank my friends who have helped me in many different ways while I have been writing this book—in particular Arun Ghosh, Stig Machin, Pat Machin, Jo Thomas, Matthew Francis, Christine Howitt, Elaine Hepburn, and John Tresch.

Introduction

∽

The Place and the Path

M*ovements and Positions* first began, and now begins again, with questions about inwardness. This is an essential category for Kierkegaard: "in inwardness" qualifies many of his descriptions of personal, existential truth or authenticity, and applies specifically to the sphere of religious faith. "In a spiritual sense, the place and the path are within a man, and just as the place is the blessed state of the striving soul, so the path is the striving soul's continual transformation."[1] From the perspective of "the task of becoming a Christian" invoked by Kierkegaard's writing, inwardness is, it seems, the most important part of a human being.

So I started to wonder, *what is inwardness?* What kind of place is it, and where does its path lead to? What exactly happens there, and how? If we could 'get inside' and explore inwardness, what would it look like? These are not easy questions, because one of the most important features of Kierkegaardian inwardness is its privacy—its secrecy, its incommunicability, its solitude. "True inwardness demands absolutely no outward sign."[2] Inwardness is where the individual relates to God; it is the hidden inner sanctum of the self where the truth of Christianity is appropriated. For Kierkegaard, this religious idea of inwardness also has profound philosophical significance, as opposing Hegel's claim that truth involves a process of externalization—as opposing, in short, the theory of mediation.

Does the very notion of inwardness imply that we can understand it only negatively—as distinct from all external things; as inaccessible through sensation, reflection or language; as inarticulate subjectivity? If so, there seems to be a danger that at the heart of Kierkegaard's interpretation of human existence lies a kind of philosophical black hole, empty of meaning and unyielding to our enquiries about the 'how' of Christian faith. It is certainly true that Kierkegaard places inwardness in some sense *beyond* reason—and many readers do, indeed, dismiss him on the grounds of his "irrationalism." As it turns out, what follows is an attempt to illuminate inwardness; to uncover the processes of its articulation through Kierkegaard's writing; and to find form or structure—or even logic—in this expression. I have discovered that *inwardness is a kind of movement*: a movement that opposes philosophical thinking, but which, nevertheless, has its own coherence and integrity.

I first came to the question of movement when I was trying to make sense of Kierkegaard's opposition to Hegel's account of the relationship between "the internal" and "the external." While considering the reasons for Kierkegaard's vehement and sustained attack on Hegel, I was drawn to one particularly intriguing criticism: the suggestion that *there is no movement in Hegel's philosophy*.[3] What, I wondered, could Kierkegaard mean by this? What kind of movement might be expected of a philosophy—and why is this important?

Reading Kierkegaard's *Repetition* with these questions in mind, I soon began to see movements everywhere. *Repetition* starts with a reference to a debate among ancient Greek philosophers about the possibility of motion and then introduces the idea of repetition as a movement that opposes the Platonic doctrine of recollection. In this text, movement is not only a subject for philosophical discussion (a discussion that includes explicit criticism of Hegelian mediation), but is also employed in a more literary way to describe different forms of consciousness and the transitions between them. In *Fear and Trembling*, again, Kierkegaard speaks of faith as a "leap," and tells the story of Abraham's journey to illustrate the "double movement" of resignation and faith. What, then, is the connection between these metaphors of movement and the suggestion that there is no movement in Hegel's philosophy? What does movement signify for Kierkegaard, and where—and how—do his movements take place? Strangely enough, these questions lead back to my enquiry about the meaning of inwardness: Kierkegaardian movement expresses intensification, and this dynamic intensity turns out to be synonymous with inwardness. Man's inner place is "the blessed state of the striving soul," and his path is this soul's "continual transformation." If inwardness is not really a "place" at all (since it is opposed precisely to anything extended), but a movement, then exploring the theme of movement will reveal something of the hidden interiority that constitutes, for Kierkegaard, the sphere of "becoming a Christian." What follows is an attempt to address the question, *what is the significance of movement in Kierkegaard's writing?*

In a way, it is not at all surprising to find metaphors of movement in Kierkegaard's texts, for the idea of an individual's relationship to God as a kind of inward journey or pilgrimage has prevailed throughout the Christian tradition. Augustine, for example, begins his *Confessions* by proclaiming that "Our hearts, O Lord, are restless until they find their rest in you." Furthermore, the historical consciousness that infused philosophical and theological thinking at the beginning of the nineteenth century drew attention to the way in which the truth is *in process*; to the way in which truth is affected—and perhaps even *effected*—by time. Hegel's *Phenomenology of Spirit*, published in 1807 (six years before Kierkegaard was born), describes the dialectical development and expression of collective self-consciousness, the "Absolute Spirit." So when Kierkegaard writes about "the stages on life's way" this echoes a metaphor running through both the Christian tradition and the most recent philosophy.

The "existentialist" perspective that Kierkegaard brings to the spheres of philosophy and faith accentuates the priority of becoming over being: the priority of freedom and action ("the ethical") over reflection and knowledge ("the aesthetic"). "Ethics does not have the medium of *being* but the medium of *becoming*."[4] Kierkegaard is profoundly influenced by Hegel's emphasis on temporality as the form of truth, but he insists that this is most significant from the point of view of the particular individual's self-consciousness, rather than the universal consciousness of Absolute Spirit. "I live in time. An existing individual is himself in a process of becoming," insists the pseudonym Johannes Climacus.[5]

Nowhere is this process of becoming more important to Kierkegaard than in the sphere of Christian faith. For Kierkegaard, indeed, Christianity only has truth as a way of living in relationship to God, as the individual's subjective faith. He speaks not of *being* a Christian, but of *becoming* a Christian. Given that questions about becoming have, at least since their articulation by ancient Greek philosophers, led to questions about motion and change, we might expect Kierkegaard to be interested in movement.

In Kierkegaard's *Repetition* movement is thematized in a much more complete way than in texts such as Aristotle's *Physics* and *Metaphysics*,

Augustine's *Confessions*, or Hegel's *Phenomenology of Spirit*. In *Repetition*—one of three quite astonishing pseudonymous works which, published in 1843, mark the beginning of Kierkegaard's authorship—movement is significant at every level of the text. This book introduces itself as concerned with a kind of movement called repetition, which is supposed to constitute a new philosophical category. Historically, in raising the question of motion it addresses itself to ancient Greek metaphysics (in particular to Aristotle) and to Hegelian philosophy, and also to more recent debates about Aristotle and Hegel among Kierkegaard's contemporaries. On a more poetic level, the theme of movement (and stasis) is expressed through the text's metaphors, characters, and dramatic structure. The communicative techniques of Kierkegaard's writing—that is, the way in which he addresses his readers and seeks to affect them—are again concerned with certain kinds of movement. From a biographical perspective, too, movement emerges as having a personal significance for Kierkegaard: metaphors of movement and questions about motion pervade his journals during the early 1840s, often in the context of reflections on love, on studying philosophy, or on becoming a Christian. Kierkegaard's grasp of his own inner life *in terms of the question of motion* helps to illuminate his personal relationship to his published writings.

Kierkegaard's interest in movement reflects his ambivalent attitude toward philosophy. He opposes existential becoming to intellectual reflection, but in raising questions of motion he steps into an ongoing philosophical debate that is rooted in the Greek origins of metaphysics. This means that in order to understand the significance of the theme of movement that recurs throughout Kierkegaard's work, we must first consider why and how movement became a question for philosophy. As it turns out, the two thinkers who are most pivotal within the tradition opened up by this question are also those philosophers who influenced Kierkegaard most strongly: Aristotle and Hegel.

I have divided *Movements and Positions* into three parts that can broadly be described as "History," "Commentary," and "Analysis." The three chapters in part 1 provide the historical, philosophical, and biographical background that a proper understanding of the theme of movement in the 1843 texts requires. Chapter 1 considers how movement first became a question for philosophy, exploring pre-Socratic debates about motion before discussing in some detail the concepts that were created by Aristotle in order to make sense of becoming. Chapter 2 traces the development of the philosophical question of movement after Aristotle, racing very selectively through medieval, early modern, and enlightenment thought to the beginning of the nineteenth century. Here we pause to consider more carefully the impact of Hegel's dynamic logic. In chapter 3 the historical focus is narrowed to Denmark in the 1830s, when Kierkegaard was studying philosophy and theology at the University of Copenhagen—an experience that affected him emotionally, even spiritually, as well as intellectually, for he often complained of the stasis and incapacity of academic life. During this period several of Kierkegaard's teachers and acquaintances were engaged in debates about Hegel's principle of mediation and Aristotelian logic, and recently translated contributions to these debates help to illuminate the significance of movement in Kierkegaard's writing.

Because addressing our question involves considering the various aspects of the theme of movement, and the ways in which they cohere, quite a substantial proportion of this book is devoted to close readings of particular texts. The historical and biographical perspectives illuminated by the question of motion have encouraged me to focus on the year 1843—for this enables us to grasp how Kierkegaard's authorship develops in response to both academic and personal concerns with movement. Concentrating on the 1843 texts also accentuates the way in which *Either/Or*, *Repetition*, and *Fear and Trembling* form a trilogy connected by the theme of movement, and by a preoccupation with "the task of becoming a Christian" which on the whole remains implicit. In part 2, chapters 4, 5, and 6 present readings of these three texts, and in each case Kierkegaard's writing is approached primarily as literature rather than as philosophy or theology. This helps to maintain an openness to the texts which, in the end, affords a deeper appreciation of the religious and philosophical questions that they raise.

Questions, metaphors, and dramatizations of movement continue to resonate in Kierkegaard's writing after 1843, so that the commentaries in part 2 illuminate the variations on the theme of movement that appear in subsequent texts, and the research presented in part 1 provides a context for the authorship as a whole. This allows us to return, in part 3, to the notion of inwardness with new insight into its coherence, its truth, and its power as the reciprocal movement of divine grace and finite love. The movements uncovered in Kierkegaard's writing at once subvert philosophy's traditional project of knowledge and create a new metaphysics of the heart. The inward essence that empowers beings—the 'thing-in-itself' that Hegel had expelled from thought—is rediscovered by Kierkegaard in the intensive and yet relational movement of spiritual passion. As Deleuze suggests, Kierkegaard's project is "to put metaphysics in motion, in action"—and this movement has since been repeated, in very diverse ways, by Nietzsche, Heidegger, and Deleuze himself.

The aim of this book is, above all, to present a coherent interpretation of the 1843 texts, informed by their intellectual context, that brings clarity to Kierkegaard's enigmatic and often difficult authorship. Focusing on the theme of movement illuminates many of the questions raised by this authorship: questions about Kierkegaard's relationship to the philosophical tradition and to philosophical thinking in general; about the meaning of the famous claim that "subjectivity is truth"; about the "how" of Christian faith; about the polemical and edifying intentions of Kierkegaard's writing—for as existing individuals, we are invited to think about movement in order to encounter ourselves in a new way, according to a new mode of valuation, a new form of truth.

Part One

Chapter One

∞

Metaphysics of Motion

"The task of becoming a Christian" is the problem and the purpose of Kierkegaard's whole authorship, and the "becoming" in question here is not incidental or external to its "task" of Christianity, but rather essential to it. A Christian is after all an existing individual, and to exist means to be inescapably in a process of becoming. Kierkegaard's concern is about *how* this human becoming is to be channeled toward Christianity: what does it mean to become a Christian, and how is this possible?

Questions about the significance and possibility of becoming have a history as old as philosophy itself. The concept of becoming that has been discussed and developed throughout this history has its roots in the Greek *kinesis*, which translates into English as both movement and change. The experience of becoming, of the emergence and passing away of things, was to ancient minds a source of the wonder that led them to seek insight into the powers at work in the world. The philosophical tradition has since remained preoccupied with comprehending and articulating the unfolding, *kinetic* nature of existence. Kierkegaard's enquiry into becoming from the perspective of the task of Christianity is, of course, positioned rather differently from the Greeks' attempts to make sense of the *cosmos*—but the revival of these earliest debates about the possibility of motion is integral to his project of creating an 'existentialist' philosophy. In particular, Aristotle's theories and categories, which were developed above all in order to account for kinesis, provided Kierkegaard with a conceptual framework that could be adapted to his own analysis of religious becoming. If we want to understand the significance of movement both for philosophy in general and for Kierkegaard in particular, the ancient Greek metaphysics of motion is the best place to begin.

Heraclitus taught that everything is constantly in motion, at once coming into being and passing away, flowing like "an ever-living fire." This philosophy of flux means that the appearance of solid, individual things is an illusion and leads to the conclusion that knowledge is impossible. This tension between movement and knowledge proved to be the greatest problem (*aporia*: literally, difficulty of passage) in Greek thought: although we see things moving around and changing, how are we to conceive of this logically? If something is now one way and then another, is there a moment when it is neither? Or when it is both? And how can something come into being when it is preceded by nothing? If something changes, in what sense is it still the same thing?

One solution to the aporia of becoming, favored by the Eleatic school of philosophers, was to claim that change is impossible and thus unreal. Parmenides's poem *Way of Truth* argues that "what is" is one and indivisible, subject neither to coming to be nor to destruction. Here the pursuit of knowledge and its requirement of intelligibility override the evidence of sense perception. Indeed, both Heraclitus and Parmenides approach the question of motion by suggesting that things are not as they appear to be: one denies the reality of enduring individual things, and the other denies the reality of their movement. The mystery of becoming provides an impulse to metaphysics by making appearances questionable.

Plato's more sophisticated ontology in a way combines the views of Heraclitus and the Eleatics. Plato agrees with the former that the physical world is a flowing stream of becoming that cannot yield knowledge of the truth, but he avoids Heraclitus's skeptical conclusions by positing, like Parmenides, a superior reality that is eternal, unchanging, and intelligible. For Plato, the realm of Forms or Ideas is "*really* real," whereas apparent, particular things, "tossed about" between being and not-being, are like mere shadows of what properly exists. This view of becoming as a lesser kind of being means that a philosopher's priority is to contemplate the Forms rather than to investigate kinesis. Plato does provide some discussion of movement: notably, in the *Laws* he distinguishes ten kinds of motion, ending with "life" that moves both itself and other things. This concept of life as the source of motion is used to argue that the soul, as the giver of life, is immortal; and in the *Timaeus* God is portrayed as the "best soul," the self-moved mover of the best motions. However, throughout Plato's works the movements of souls are subordinated to the Form of the Good, and he does not offer what we, since Aristotle, would recognize as a full account of motion.

Aristotle is the first philosopher to be committed equally to the intelligibility of the world and to the reality of movement. In all fields of enquiry, his investigations aim as far as possible to explain the *phenomena* (not only the appearances of things, but also common opinions about them) that present themselves to experience, and he is dismissive of the Eleatics' attempt to refute the self-evident fact of motion:

> The first of those who studied philosophy were misled in their search for the truth and the nature of things by their inexperience, which as it were thrust them into another path. So they say that none of the things that are either comes to be or passes out of existence, because what comes to be must do so either from what is or from what is not, both of which are impossible.[1]

Aristotle addresses more seriously the materialist theories of change that had been proposed as an alternative to Parmenides's denial of movement: he argues that viewing all kinesis as a rearrangement of atoms fails to account for qualitative change. Above all, though, Aristotle's investigations of the cosmos under the titles of *Physics* and *Metaphysics* are concerned to show that the dualistic ontology offered by Plato's doctrine of the Forms cannot provide a satisfactory explanation of becoming.

∞

For Aristotle, wisdom consists in "knowledge of primary causes and principles": while Plato's philosophical enquiry aims to establish the definitions or essences of beings, through reference to transcendent Forms, Aristotle is committed also to explaining how things operate. He is interested in the processes of nature, and particularly in causation; by distinguishing between different kinds of causes, and between different categories of being, he attempts to articulate and to analyze the powers of becoming. In his *Metaphysics* Aristotle offers many objections to Platonic Forms, but suggests that their most serious weakness is their failure to account for kinesis: "Above all we might examine the question of what on earth the Forms contribute to sensible things . . . for they are not the cause of any motion or change in them."[2] This criticism of Platonic idealism helps to illuminate the significance of Aristotle's philosophy for Kierkegaard, because it provides a parallel to his existentialist critique of Hegelian thought. In 1841 Kierkegaard recorded this quotation from the *Metaphysics* in his notes on Schelling's lectures, adding that "Aristotle . . . censures those who want to grasp actuality *en tois logois*. He censures

Plato's doctrine of the participation of things in the ideas and calls this *kenologein* [using empty words]."[3] Kierkegaard, like Aristotle, argues that Ideas alone cannot cause movement and cannot account for actuality; both thinkers counteract idealism by searching for a source of motion *within* existing things.

Aristotle begins his treatise on *Physics* by identifying things that "exist by nature," or "have a nature," as those beings that have in themselves a principle of motion and rest. Nature (*phusis*) is "a cause that operates for a purpose"; a process of development toward a *telos*. Aristotle emphasizes that "nature is always in a subject (*hypokeimenon*)," which means that this autonomous sort of motion takes place on the basis of an underlying, relatively enduring thing. Unlike previous philosophers, he views movement as the inner activity of things, as their "innate impulse to change." For Plato, this inner power is flighty: the winged soul for a while sacrifices its freedom in order to animate a body, but always leaves this behind again in its pursuit of higher things. Aristotle is more inclined to accept finitude, and this allows him to achieve a deeper analysis of worldly beings.

Having defined nature in terms of teleological movement and change, Aristotle goes on to offer a more precise account of kinesis. He introduces some clarity into the debates over the aporia of becoming by emphasizing the distinction between "potentiality," *dunamis*, and "actuality," *energeia*. The Greek dunamis can mean power, capacity, or even faculty (Aristotle refers to the dunameis of the soul), and energeia signifies activity, fulfillment—but here these terms are used to crystallize aspects of the process of natural development. For example, a seed is 'potentially' what the mature plant is 'actually'; bronze and the sculptor's craft together provide the potentiality of a statue, which is actualized during the formation of the figure. There is some correspondence between potentiality and actuality, and matter and form, but the former opposition makes explicit the dynamic quality of beings. Actualities, or forms, are not transcendent and separate entities, as conceived by Plato, but rather are gradually brought into being during a process of change. Aristotle suggests that his predecessors' difficulties in making sense of kinesis were due to the fact that it can be classified as neither potentiality nor actuality: movement must be understood as the passage from one to the other. "Motion is an incomplete fulfillment of the movable"; "motion occurs just when the fulfillment itself occurs, and neither before nor after." Kinesis is, then, a category of transition, and it signifies a process of actualization.

In a sense, Aristotle's entire philosophy can be viewed as responsive to the question of movement. The concepts integral to his ontology each provide a kind of anchor for his vision of becoming: not only his analysis of causation and his distinction between potentiality and actuality, but also his doctrines of substance and soul, his principles of logic, and his notion of God function to make intelligible the processes of the cosmos. Aristotle's categories of being—substance, quality, quantity, relation, position, and so on—are used to distinguish different kinds of change and to prevent confusion between them: ruling out the possibility of transition from nothing to something in the category of substance (so that the cosmos as a whole cannot have come into being, and must therefore be eternal) does not mean that we have to deny qualitative becoming, growth, or locomotion.

Aristotle makes use of his concepts of potentiality and actuality to define both God and the soul. He describes the soul, rather obscurely, as "an actuality of the first kind of a natural body having life potentially in it." A human soul can be identified with its various dunameis such as growth, sensation, locomotion, desire, and reason, and these constitute the life force of the individual. Aristotle's doctrine of the soul provides the link between his physics and his theology, for the motions of the soul tend purposefully toward God as the sustaining principle of the cosmos as a whole.

For Aristotle, God occupies a necessary role as the ultimate source of motion—not because the cosmos requires a creator but, on the contrary, because its processes can only be conceived as eternal: "since there must be motion without intermission, there must necessarily be something eternal . . . that first imparts motion, and this first mover must be unmoved." Aristotle's insistence in the *Metaphysics* that God is himself unmoved aims to provide an explanatory first cause that will prevent further questions as to the source of *his* movement, but this argument is also supported by the distinction between potentiality and actuality. The primary source of motion in the cosmos must be actual, for something that merely has a potential need not exercise it, and this is inconsistent with the eternity of movement. Because God must be fully actual, he must also be unmoved given that motion implies potentiality; something undergoes change *insofar* as it possesses the potential to do so.

How can something move without being moved? Aristotle suggests that "the object of desire and the object of thought move in this way": these are "final causes" of movement by virtue of their goodness (apparently good in the case of desire, and really good in the case of thought). An example of an unmoved mover, or final cause, is a big cream cake in the window of a baker's shop: motionless, it moves a passer-by into the shop to buy herself a cake. Of course, this is merely an apparent good, whereas the final cause of all motion in the universe must be a real good from every point of view.

This objective good is, for Aristotle, the perfect order and proper functioning of the cosmos. God is himself this order (*logos*); he is an eternal mind or rather an eternal act of thinking that comprehends the order of everything. Aristotle posits at the heart of the cosmos a full, unending activity that secures its intelligibility by causing things consistently to behave, to *become*, in the way they do. Typically keen to ground philosophical knowledge on sense experience, Aristotle finds evidence of this God in the visible circular motions of "the heavens"—the planets, the stars, and the sun.

Aristotle's God is not a personal being that moves things around at will, directing events in the world, but rather the cosmos moves as a response to God. Individual things respond to God by realizing themselves; a desire for realization is built into the soul as an aspect of its essential nature. The actualizing movements of beings are 'toward God' not in the sense of a religious relationship, but in the sense that the repeated becoming of particular individuals perpetuates the species, so that each finite thing contributes to a reflection of eternity. We can see how it is natural for Aristotle to see rational thought as the highest activity of human life: our self-realization involves grasping the eternal laws or principles of the dynamic being that God sustains. (This idea echoes throughout the history of philosophy, becoming particularly resonant in Spinoza's *Ethics* and then in Hegel's speculative thought.)

In Book IV of the *Metaphysics*, Aristotle sets out those principles that, as the laws of both nature and thought, must ground the science of "being as being." The most certain of all principles is, he suggests, that "the same attribute cannot at the same time belong and not belong to the same subject in the same respect." This rule has become known as the principle of contradiction, and for Aristotle it secures the possibility of intelligible discourse: he argues that no one can deny its validity, since as soon as we say anything at all we refer to something that cannot at the same time be something else. Without such a principle, meaning would always remain uncertain. (Of course, in the past few decades several philosophers have affirmed this insecurity of meaning and seem to be quite happy about it. This wasn't an option for Aristotle, though, because his task was to create concepts that could make some sense of a mysterious world. Only because the rational order that he helped to articulate has now become entrenched have more recent writers desired to overcome it.) Aristotle states his principle of contradiction in order to establish that the terms "to be" and "not to be" have a definite meaning—and this is essential to his account of movement, for he is here opposing views such as those of Heraclitus, which "do away with substance and essence."

Aristotle insists that there must be an underlying thing that persists through change, and that kinesis is the transition between two states that are meaningfully distinct from one another.

So for Aristotle, the intelligibility of movement as well as of substance relies on the logical principle of contradiction. This philosophical issue provides one important starting point of our enquiry, for it establishes a trajectory leading directly to Hegel, and on to Kierkegaard. To anticipate: when Hegel developed his dialectical method, he was attempting to formalize a kind of reasoning more dynamic than the traditional, Aristotelian laws of logic allow, which could more adequately express the dynamic truth of becoming. While Aristotle's logic is based on contradiction (thesis and antithesis), Hegel introduces a triadic form wherein contradiction is mediated by a third, synthetic term. Aristotle, Hegel, and Kierkegaard all agree that contradiction is a condition of movement. However, they have different interpretations of the significance of contradiction: for Aristotle, it *identifies* the thing that moves and the stages of its progress; for Hegel, it leads to a *mediation* of concepts that propels the process of reasoning—and also, ultimately, the development of consciousness itself; for Kierkegaard, it grounds *choice* in the sphere of ethical freedom. As we shall see, Kierkegaard's argument against Hegel returns to Aristotle's insistence that contradiction is final and irreconcilable: he claims that Hegel dissolves differences and oppositions through his dialectical conflation of becoming and rationality, so that only a semblance of motion is possible within his speculative philosophy.

∞

Kierkegaard began to study Aristotle seriously in 1841, when at the age of twenty-eight he went to Berlin after breaking off his engagement to Regine Olsen. While living in Berlin, attending lectures on philosophy and writing *Either/Or*, Kierkegaard further distracted himself from Regine by working his way through W. G. Tenneman's weighty *Geschichte der Philosophie*. This contained a thorough exposition of Aristotle's philosophy, and after Kierkegaard's return to Copenhagen in March 1842 his journal entries begin to reflect his increasing interest in Aristotle—and especially in the concept of kinesis. Kierkegaard was intrigued by Aristotle's view of movement and change as the fulfillment of that which exists potentially. He notes that

> the transition from potentiality to actuality is a change [Danish: *forandring*, German *veranderung*]—thus Tenneman translates *kinesis*; if this is correct, this sentence is of the utmost importance. *Kinesis* is difficult to

define, because it belongs neither to possibility nor to actuality, is more than possibility and less than actuality.

A little later he adds that "Hegel has never done justice to the category of transition. It would be significant to compare it with the Aristotelian teaching about *kinesis*." Aristotle became an influential force in Kierkegaard's developing thought because he offered a philosophical discussion of motion that helped to illuminate Kierkegaard's intuition that Hegel's system could not fully accommodate the process of becoming that characterizes existence. No doubt Kierkegaard was acutely aware at this time of the changes going on in his own life, as he grieved for Regine and for his father, and wrestled with questions about his religious and literary vocation.

As Kierkegaard continued his study of Aristotle (often under the guidance of the German logician Trendelenburg, whose work he discovered in 1844), he came to appreciate the importance of the whole conceptual structure of kinesis. As we have seen, Aristotle uses the term 'potentiality,' dunamis, to express a capacity for movement. Kinesis, as the transition from potentiality to actuality, signifies a process of actualization. The accomplishment of Hegelian logic is to mediate this process of actualization, to explicate becoming according to necessary formal laws. Kierkegaard argues, however, that because mediation operates necessarily and immanently—"within reason, within history, within the Hegelian system"—it is not really a *process* at all. More specifically, it is an illusory process, because although it expresses a progression in thought it lacks any power of becoming: *it lacks freedom*. It is this freedom, says Kierkegaard, which makes the transition from potentiality to actuality a real event, a genuine movement, a qualitative change. And this brings us back to Aristotle's definition of kinesis. Kierkegaard's understanding of human freedom draws on this concept of kinesis as expressing an actualizing power, a kind of capability of becoming. This is illustrated very concisely by his remark, recorded in his journal, that "freedom means to be capable."

This is not to suggest that Kierkegaard simply opposes Aristotle's account of motion to Hegel's. In order to juxtapose, to compare, or to oppose to one another different philosophers' interpretations of movement, we must take into account the basic *position* or locality of each particular account of becoming. That is, we have to ask first of all, *what kind of movement is in question here?*—and even more simply, *what moves? where to?*—before we can raise the question of *how* this motion occurs. In thus describing movements we tend to find ourselves using spatial metaphors: we might say that for Aristotle *the sphere within which* the power of movement operates is the cosmos, the totality of beings made intelligible through an ontology of substance and a logic of contradiction. We could call this 'position' a sphere, realm, region, locale, plane, or even theater of motion. 'Plane of motion' is perhaps the most neutral metaphor, although we must remain aware that its spatiality is indeed metaphorical—at least in the case of certain 'planes.'

'Plane of motion' is a useful expression for several reasons. It helps to clarify comparisons between different accounts of motion: some may operate on the same plane, while others may involve certain fundamental modifications, or even the emergence of a new plane. This will enable us to explore within the context of the philosophical tradition Kierkegaard's thematization of movement *on the plane of existential inwardness*. Transferring certain concepts from Aristotle's metaphysics onto this subjective plane does not make Kierkegaard an Aristotelian, just as occupying a plane that overlaps with Hegel's does not make him Hegelian, and only by understanding this can we begin to make sense of his philosophical position in relation to Aristotle, to Hegel, and to other thinkers. Speaking of a plane of motion may also help us to *visualize* a particular philosophy in its entirety, in its coherence (if it has one). Most importantly, the concept of a plane of motion invokes the question of ground, of truth—to every plane of motion belongs a process of articulation, something like a 'logic' of power expressed—without imposing a single, generalizing logical standard. Our plane of motion owes something to Heidegger's notion of a "clearing" (*lichtung*) or "region" of Being, and also to Deleuze's "plane of immanence," elucidated in *What Is Philosophy?*—though these provide inspiration rather than any kind of precise conceptual grounding. Indeed, this is integral to the spirit of both Heidegger and Deleuze, for each seeks a way of speaking about philosophy that avoids such methodological presuppostions. The meaning and significance of the plane of motion will become increasingly clear through its application, from time to time, as we consider the diverse interpretations of movement offered by Kierkegaard, Hegel, Aristotle, and others.

The plane of motion changes radically during the history of philosophy from Aristotle through to Hegel. Aristotle's enquiry into kinesis seeks to understand the natural world and the order of its processes. On this plane, motions are envisaged as circular, like the heavens, and the relative dimensions of 'external' and 'internal' correspond to physical, sensible beings and their inner principles, potencies, or causes of change. In contrast to Aristotle's scientific and naturalistic position, Kierkegaard inherits from Hegel a spiritual plane of motion, formed by temporality, subjectivity, and reflexivity, and of course profoundly affected by Christianity. However, Kierkegaard departs crucially from Hegel in locating this plane *within* each existing individual, which alters the perspective entirely. The dynamic self-consciousness that Hegel investigates so thoroughly in its logical and world-historical proportions becomes identified with individuality as *inwardness*. Kierkegaard wants to bring Aristotle's concept of a real transition *into* the realm of inwardness, of the heart's potency, in order to secure its freedom. "Both in his critique of Hegel and in his search for a concept that could serve as the basis for his dynamic, projective conception of human existence, Kierkegaard seized on Aristotle's concept of kinesis, applying it, characteristically, exclusively to man's becoming."[4] Kierkegaard's task is to transfer the Aristotelian concept of kinesis to a plane of motion that has become synonymous with selfhood; to recreate this actualizing movement according to a 'position' constituted by existential subjectivity and by a Christian consciousness.

∞

The commentaries on Kierkegaard's first pseudonymous publications presented in part 2 will uncover this aspect of his authorship. Because Aristotle, like Hegel, is not discussed explicitly and extensively by the pseudonyms until Johannes Climacus's *Philosophical Fragments* (1844) and *Concluding Unscientific Postscript* (1846), it is worth looking to these texts for illustrations of Kierkegaard's use and adaptation of Aristotelian ideas. This will help to clarify in a preliminary way the significance of kinesis for the 1843 publications, and so for the development of Kierkegaard's religious existentialism.

As we have seen, Aristotle's philosophy aims to render intelligible movement and change. By insisting on an underlying subject that persists through change, and an "unmoved mover" to which all finite motions can be referred, Aristotle grounds the possibility of a change that is both qualitative and real, securing the distinct power of individual movements. This distinctiveness and individuality is in turn consolidated by the logical principle of contradiction. Aristotle uses the concept of something that is itself unchangeble and static to give coherence to the movements of particular things—and this seems essential because Heraclitus's view that everything is in motion leads to an aporia in making sense of change. Johannes Climacus echoes this in an important passage in *Concluding Unscientific Postscript*:

> In so far as existence consists in movement there must be something which can give continuity to the movement and hold it together, for otherwise there is no movement. Just as the assertion that everything is

true means that nothing is true, so the assertion that everything is in motion means that there is no motion. The unmoved is therefore a constituent of motion as its measure and its end. Otherwise the assertion that everything is in motion, is *ipso facto* an assertion of a state of rest. Aristotle, who emphasises movement in so many ways, therefore says that God, himself unmoved, moves all.[5]

Although Climacus here agrees with Aristotle that motion requires some factor of constancy, he does not want to locate this constancy in an unchanging God. Aristotelian movement takes place on a cosmological plane, and God at the center of this cosmos provides the eternal element of stability. Climacus, however, wants to find a source of movement within a human being—but he cannot posit the stability of eternity here: "the difficulty facing an existing individual is how to give his existence the continuity without which everything simply vanishes . . . the very existence of the existing individual is sufficient to prevent his continuity from having essential stability." Lacking the eternal being of God, the individual has to anchor and empower the movement of his consciousness in some other way. The *intensity* of passion, pushed to its maximum by Christian faith (which, Climacus emphasises, concerns the believer's *eternal* happiness), functions as a kind of finite approximation to eternity:

> Passion gives [the individual] a momentary continuity, a continuity which at one and the same time is a restraining influence and a moving impulse. The goal of movement for an existing individual is to arrive at a decision, and to renew it. The eternal is the factor of continuity; but an abstract eternity is extraneous to the movement of life, and a concrete eternity within the existing individual is the maximum degree of his passion. All idealizing passion is an anticipation of the eternal in existence, functioning so as to help the individual to exist.[6]

Climacus's criticism of the notion of "an abstract eternity" here is directed at Hegelian philosophy. Passion, he argues, is concrete and actual insofar as it has real power. Because its continuity is "momentary," passion is preserved only through renewal: a relationship to a loved one (whether human or divine) is not achieved 'once and for all,' but at every moment. Throughout his authorship, Kierkegaard emphasizes that faith is always a task, always a movement, not a state one attains in order to find repose.

For Kierkegaard, the Greeks' philosophical question about the possibility of motion becomes a religious question of *how* the task of Christianity is to be undertaken. Whereas Aristotle insists that kinesis requires a substance that endures the process of becoming, Johannes Climacus claims in *Philosophical Fragments* that a qualitative transition occurs only "if that which comes into existence *does not in itself remain unchanged* in the process of coming into existence." This indicates that Kierkegaard's perspective of existential subjectivity involves the rejection of Aristotle's substantialist ontology. But if Aristotle needed a concept of substance to ground the coherence of kinesis, how can Kierkegaard account for movement without lapsing back into Heraclitus's denial of individuality? Or to put it another way, what is the basis of individuality if existence is, without exception, becoming? This question takes us to the heart of the matter, for in order to address it we must consider the Christian consciousness that underpins Kierkegaard's exploration of these philosophical issues.

Climacus contends that, in the individual's transition to Christianity, the basis of the self does *not* remain unchanged. He pushes the concept of qualitative movement further than Aristotle, so that *kinesis* becomes the "double movement" of Christianity. The individual's leap of faith requires a complete transformation of existence; it is the basis of existence itself that is transformed, so that everything upon this basis is renewed. In becoming truly religious the individual gives up the worldly basis of his consciousness, and instead grounds his entire existence in his relationship to God. Human life, suggests Kierkegaard, is not characterized by substantiality: we do not exist independently; we cannot understand ourselves on our own terms; and if we attempt to do so, we are committing an error which, according to Christian doctrine, amounts to sin. Becoming a Christian involves the realization that one owes one's *actual, becoming* existence to God, and that this truth can only be expressed through a life of faith and thankfulness towards Him.

From his Christian perspective, Kierkegaard transforms Aristotle's account of kinesis as grounded in substance, while retaining his understanding of movement in terms of a process of actualization (particular 'hearts' or 'souls' are empowered with the dunamis of existential becoming). Something similar happens to Aristotle's concept of God as the "unmoved mover": although it finds some sort of approximation in human passion, this pagan deity can have no place in a theology of transcendence and incarnation. Just as the significance of eternity is concentrated within the existing individual as passion, so the power of God is concentrated, particularized, into a human form: the transformation of the individual—the task of becoming religious—is conditioned by the transformation of God. According to Christian teaching this happened once in history, when God incarnated Himself in the life of Jesus. (Though according to

Nietzsche, a subsequent transformation had to follow, for a living God must eventually die.) For Kierkegaard, the miraculous, paradoxical logic of the Christian incarnation eclipses Aristotle's understanding of God as an eternal unmoved mover. In the *Postscript* Climacus suggests (in what seems like a rather Hegelian fashion) that the pagan relationship to God was too ideal—too objective, too external, too *aesthetic*—to facilitate the existential movement that Jesus calls upon his followers to make. Climacus draws our attention to the difference between Aristotle's God, and the God who in becoming a man changes His own being:

> The existential sphere of paganism is essentially the aesthetic, and hence it is quite in order for the pagan consciousness to be reflected in the conception of God which holds that He, Himself unchanged, changes all. This is the expression for outwardly directed action. The religious lies in the dialectic of inwardness, and hence it is sympathetic with the conception of God that He is Himself moved, changed.[7]

This does not mean that Kierkegaard rejects the idea of an eternal, constant, unchanging God—indeed, several of his "Edifying Discourses" meditate on "The Unchangeableness of God." Instead, Kierkegaard repeatedly emphasizes that God's eternity and His historical coming into existence occur alongside one another. This intersection of eternity and temporality is precisely the contradiction, the paradox, which makes the Christian incarnation miraculous, and which requires the individual to make a leap of faith in order to relate to God. Unlike the accounts of self-realization offered by most philosophers—and notably by Hegel and Aristotle—Kierkegaard's "task of becoming a Christian" is not an intellectual act. Christ is encountered as a paradoxical revelation which excites passionate, decisive commitment: a movement of *intensification* in which the individual's consciousness is "raised to the second power," and her life takes on a higher significance through its direct, personal relationship to God. The freedom of this movement is encountered existentially as a repeated renewal of the moment of choice, and as a repeated transformation of the self.

Kierkegaard found in Aristotle's philosophy a conceptual structure that anchors movement in reality. Aristotle is always concerned to make human experience intelligible and rational. This may appear to be antithetical to Kierkegaard's approach insofar as he challenges the supremacy of reason—and as we have seen, Aristotle's account of motion undergoes significant modification through its relocation to the plane of existential subjectivity. However, it is also true to say that Kierkegaard sought to make intelligible, both to himself and others, some of his most personal experiences (such as his sense of impotence with regard to committing to Christianity or to marriage), and to articulate the inward processes involved in these existential movements. Aristotle's solutions to the problem of kinesis provided for Kierkegaard a philosophical framework within which to clarify the nature of transitions within the realm of subjective, religious becoming—and also, more intimately, to explore the movements going on within his own troubled soul.

Chapter Two

The Logic of Becoming

For Aristotle, movement is understood in terms of *actualization*. The concept of phusis signifies a potentiality, a potency, a *power* for movement, and kinesis is defined as the process through which this power is expressed. Crucially, kinesis is an *inner power* that grounds the individuality of existing things. This concept of power echoes repeatedly throughout the subsequent history of philosophy, although it assumes various guises—for example, Spinoza's *conatus*; Kant's 'thing in itself'; Nietzsche's 'will to power.' Aristotle's God, the 'unmoved mover' or 'final cause' of all things, is the ultimate source of power, and the laws of logic are identical with the operations of the divine mind. Thus, for Aristotle, the source of power and the logic of its expression are eternal; all motion within the cosmos is grounded by God's unceasing, completely actual affirmation of being. This idea of God's 'fullness of being' was popular among medieval theologians: Anselm and Aquinas add Aristotelian concepts to their Christian doctrine of a divine Creator and rationally defend God as "that than which nothing greater can be conceived," and as the causal ground of the universe. Aristotle's cosmological plane of motion, his metaphysics of substance, and the scientific, objective position of his enquiry into becoming remain intact through the Christian philosophies of the middle ages.

In the seventeenth century, new developments in the physical sciences were accompanied by intensified philosophical interest in the question of movement. Thomas Hobbes, for example, attempted to give an account of both the natural and social worlds on the basis of atoms and motion: he suggests that all reality emerges from the movements of bodies of the smallest size; that reasoning is a kind of motion; and that the *motions of government* generate and sustain the civil state. Hobbes's atomism provokes the same question that Aristotle raises against his materialist predecessors: how are we to account for qualitative change if everything consists of units of matter? Hobbes, like the Greek atomists, recognizes only locomotion, explaining qualitative change simply as a rearrangement of particles and concluding that nothing moves itself. Nevertheless, in *Leviathan* (1651) the notion of power dominates Hobbes's analysis of human existence: "Life itself is but motion," a striving for becoming, "a perpetual and restless desire for power after power that ceases only in death." The inner self is, as it were, submerged in this stream of material desire: the exterior motions of sense experience give rise to, or 'imagine,' interior mental motions. For Hobbes, human beings are very much formed by the world, acted upon by external material forces; their desire is reactive, and, lacking the power to change themselves, they live and die in the sort of state that a Buddhist would describe as ignorance.

Leibniz, like Hobbes, was drawn to questions of power and motion. More strongly influenced by the theories of Newton, Copernicus, Galileo, and Kepler, he attempted to provide a philosophical grounding for "*the new science of power and action*, which one might call *dynamics*." In his essay "A Specimen of Dynamics" (1695), Leibniz defines motion as "a force striving towards change," arguing that a body's "force of nature"' is more fundamental than its extension, and that "there is never any true rest in bodies." The metaphysical vision of the world elucidated in the *Theodicy* (1710) emphasizes a divine power of actualization at work in every moment of finite becoming—and for this reason Leibniz is the only modern philosopher, besides Hegel, to be mentioned in Kierkegaard's *Repetition*.

More controversial among his contemporaries than either Leibniz or Hobbes was Spinoza, whose unique perspective has profound implications for both philosophy and theology. Like the medieval theologians, Spinoza draws heavily on Aristotle's ontology, but he reaches conclusions quite opposite to Catholic doctrine. In the *Ethics* (1677) Spinoza argues that the classical concept of substance necessarily implies absolute immanence. This means that substance becomes an infinite and unique power of being that contains everything: regarding the power of thinking as an eternal, infinite "mind," and extended nature as an eternal, infinite "body," Spinoza insists that this mind and body are parallel expressions of a single substance. Although we may conceive of, and even love, this substance as divine, reason refutes all claims about a transcendent, anthropomorphic, creative God. Indeed, the arguments at the beginning of the *Ethics* accomplish a reversal of the traditional 'ontological proof' of God's existence: beginning with the fact of existence (substance) itself, Spinoza shows that some of the divine predicates—infinity, eternity, omnipotence, omniscience—necessarily apply to it.

Spinoza's ontology means that movement is part of an infinite process, and does not express the freedom of finite individuals. Only the totality is free and self-causing. However, individuality is still defined in terms of potency: a self is a power to persevere in being, and its experiences of affects such as joy and sadness register the fluctuations of this power. Spinoza defines this persistence of an individual's existence as the preservation of a ratio of motion and rest.[1]

Spinoza is significant within this little history of movement because he infuses the plane of motion with *consciousness*. Spinoza's "attribute of thought" expresses the ideational power of the totality, and while this bears some resemblance to Aristotle's notion of the divine mind, it seems to be less abstract. For Spinoza, every mind, on whatever scale, is always the *idea of* a body. Although his substantialist ontology owes much to Aristotelian concepts, he abandons the perspective of an observer trying to render intelligible the movements and changes occurring in the objects around him. That "the order and connection of ideas is the same as the order and connection of things" is a basic tenet of Spinoza's philosophy, and this integration of being and thinking within an active, infinite substance-or-subject becomes equally essential to Hegel's interpretation of motion. We may say that, in Spinoza's *Ethics*, the plane of movement becomes animated by a certain kind of subjectivity—not a Cartesian subjectivity distinct from objects and capable of doubting them, but an infinitely reflected mind that knows itself immediately as extended, as objective. Hegel's thought has absorbed this idea of concrete subjectivity, but he adds something more to the plane of motion that transforms it completely: *historicality*. If Aristotle revolutionized our understanding of movement by creating a vocabulary and a logic that allow it to be thought, Hegelian philosophy represents a second pivotal moment insofar as his logic has a principle of motion within itself. This new logos at once articulates, and is articulated by, concrete historical consciousness, or "Spirit."

∞

About one hundred years after the publication of Spinoza's *Ethics* came Kant's *Critique of Pure Reason*, which is widely recognized as accomplishing the turn to subjectivity that characterizes most nineteenth- and twentieth-century thought. The subjective consciousness uncovered by Kant's first *Critique* is transcendental: the categories of space and time, of quality, quantity, relation, causation, and so on, are *internalized* as the necessary conditions of all possible experience. These categories can be *deduced from* experience, because they are presupposed by it.

Because movement is inseparable from space and time, the Kantian revolution proposes a new plane of motion: the transcendental subject. This does not mean that the reality of movement as a power operating in the objective, external world is in any way denied, or even doubted—but the practice of speculating on this 'reality' is withdrawn from the domain of cognition. The potency for self-movement that is integral to Aristotle's concept of kinesis is precisely the 'in-itself' of things that Kant defers to a noumenal realm beyond the limits of knowledge.

This shift is not to be interpreted as neglecting or rejecting the question of kinesis. On the contrary, the dualism that results from Kant's critical project can be explained by his commitment to the intelligibility of nature's inner powers of becoming. One might ask why there have to be noumena at all—why can't Kant simply confine philosophy to our relationship with phenomena, accepting in principle Hume's skepticism and remaining content with refining it? The answer lies in Kant's concern to secure the rational order of the world. He goes further than Hume in recognizing the full implications of the fact that, *regardless of their genesis*, our ideas of causation *include their application to something real, something objective*. We *necessarily* think that if something (a phenomenon) has a cause, then that cause is not merely a phenomenon but a reality in itself. That is, appearances can only be intelligible to us on the basis of their causes—as both Aristotle and Spinoza insist—and a cause by *definition* must have reality, must have power. So for Kant the idea of a noumenon, or thing in itself, is both implicit in our understanding *and* inaccessible to knowledge. If examples of noumena are a cause and a free will, then they must be conceived in terms of power, as free, self-subsisting forces or potencies.

The subjective emphasis of Kant's critical philosophy ensures that not only the 'in-itself' of objects but also the freedom of the subject are located in the noumenal sphere. Perception and understanding become fully *active*: the faculties of cognition (or, in Aristotle's vocabulary, the dunameis of the soul) order the flux of sense data. Kant may want to "deny knowledge to make room for faith," but one effect of the first *Critique* is to transfer the world-ordering capacity—the creation of cosmos out of chaos—from God to the human subject. God may remain a permissible hypothesis as to why there is something rather than nothing, but the 'argument from design' that so appealed to Enlightenment minds (even Philo, the skeptical character in Hume's *Dialogues Concerning Natural Religion*, admits that he finds it convincing) is rendered superfluous by transcendental idealism. Legislative power, too, is now attributed to human beings: ethical action is defined purely in terms of our capacity to submit freely to the subjective, though universal, moral law. Beyond the limits of knowledge, this free will is posited as an Idea that Reason necessarily believes in, in order to ground ethics. By the end of the eighteenth century the fact of movement, and the power it implies, raises for philosophy the *moral* question of individual freedom, as well as the *ontological* question of nature's capacity for self-motion that was first addressed seriously by Aristotle.

Although transcendental thinking exemplifies an increasingly subjective perspective on questions of movement, from Aristotle to Kant the logic of motion remains itself atemporal and unchanging, and so in a certain sense static. For Aristotle, rationality reflects the eternal and immutable laws of the divine mind; for Spinoza, too, thinking as a whole—or the 'mind of God'—operates eternally and through necessity. And again, in the case of Kant, the transcendental principles necessarily apply to every particular mind because they precondition all experience; the subject is universally determined under the form of time prior to any individual's existence within time. Historically, too, until the nineteenth century, logic remained more or less unchanged, even for Kant. Of course, since Aristotle many philosophers have proposed variations on his ontological categories, and epistemological problems have resurfaced again and again. But, as Kant remarks in the preface to his *Critique of Pure Reason*, "since Aristotle [logic] has not required to retrace a single step ... It is remarkable also that to the present day this logic has not been able to advance a single step, and is thus to all appearances a closed and completed body of doctrine." This suggests that Hegel's transformation of logic through his dialectical method constitutes philosophy's first real turning from Aristotelian thinking.

Hegel's philosophical method is based on his recognition that, since all existence is characterized by becoming, truth itself must reflect this continual motion. Indeed, this cannot be otherwise because our thinking is inseparable from the process of actuality: as he explains in the *Encyclopaedia Logic*, "the true objectivity of thinking means that the thoughts, far from being merely ours, must at the same time be the real essence of the things." With Hegelian Reason, we are already within the noumenal realm, among beings as they are in themselves. "The content of philosophy is *actuality*," the "spirit" whose being is itself the creation of the world—"the outer and inner world of consciousness."[2] Spinoza's influence on Hegel is apparent here: one accomplishment of the *Ethics* is to overcome Cartesian skepticism by regarding extension and thought (objectivity and subjectivity) as complete, parallel expression of a single, integrated substance. Confronted with Kant's more sophisticated skepticism, Hegel follows Spinoza—but he focuses on the integration itself and regards it as dynamic, so that subject and object appear as moments within it. These 'moments' are at once logical and historical: components of a concept *and* phases of a process. Being is not eternally unified (and thus immediately knowable), but it does contain the principle of its unification, so that history can be interpreted as the teleological movement of reconciliation through which nature becomes transparent to consciousness.

In the *Phenomenology of Spirit* Hegel describes how this process unfolds concretely in the development of culture, politics, art, religion, and philosophy. He suggests in the preface to this work that his own historical time is particularly potent:

> Ours is a birth-time and a period of transition to a new era. Spirit has broken with the world it previously has inhabited and imagined, and is of a mind to submerge it in the past, and in the labor of its own transformation. Spirit is indeed never at rest, but always engaged in moving forward.

Hegel resembles Spinoza also insofar as he transfers traditional notions of God onto existence itself, considered as a whole: "Spirit is activity in the sense in which the Schoolmen already said of God that he is absolute actuosity."[3] Hegel adds, however, that the activity of Spirit involves its self-manifestation, so that it makes no sense to conceive of its power as a purely inward essence lacking process and exteriority. Aristotle's concepts of phusis (the power for self-movement) and telos (the divine final cause of motion) are for Hegel inseparable—with the crucial theological consequence that God must be immanent. Jean Hyppolite, whose interpretation of Hegel influenced a whole generation of French thinkers, including Derrida and Deleuze, emphasizes that "to replace the old metaphysics with Logic is also to sublate the viewpoint of a substrate prior to its predicates such as, for example, a transcendent God." More generally, Hegel's logic "exorcises the phantom of a thing-in-itself, which would always haunt our reflection and would limit knowledge in favor of faith and non-knowledge."[4] This insistence on the immanence of movement, and on reciprocity between dynamic inwardness and outward manifestation, is precisely what Kierkegaard's interpretation of existence seeks to undermine. For Hegel, subjectivity is an *expressive* power whose movements occur on the 'stage' of world history, whereas for Kierkegaard inward freedom is synonymous with selfhood and can find its highest expression only in the privacy of the individual's relationship to God.

For Hegel, philosophers have a particularly active role within Spirit's development toward realization. He views conceptual thought as the fullest, most transparent manifestation of Spirit's awareness and understanding of itself: this kind of thinking "penetrates the truth" and "purifies the subjective consciousness." On behalf of humanity as a whole, philosophers can use the dialectical method to comprehend themselves, their world, and its history as expressed in various cultural forms. This history includes, of course, a religious consciousness. Hegel argues that philosophy and religion share the same content, although they approach it in different ways (religious teachings are expressed through symbols rather than concepts). The dialectical logic that has been made explicit by philosophy can be found in theology too, so that philosophical insight clarifies religious truths and demonstrates their implicit rationality.

Hegelian theology is characterized by immanence and necessity. He interprets the doctrines of Creation and Incarnation as the self-disclosure of God in otherness. God is first revealed through nature, grasped as ordered and teleological but also as opposed to its creator; His second manifestation, in the human form of Jesus, overcomes this opposition in the relationship of Father and Son, two beings of the same kind. Hegel views this Christian revelation as more spiritual, more adequately expressive of God's true nature, and thus as an historical progression from Judaism. Belief in a God who creates a distinct and "unhomely" world is, for Hegel, the expression of a division within Spirit that needs to be reconciled—Christ manifests the "implicitly subsisting unity of divine and human nature":

> The substantial relationship of man to God *seems* to be in its truth a *beyond*, but the love of God to man and of man to God overcomes the separation of the 'Here' and the 'Now' from what is represented as a Beyond, and is *eternal life*. This identity is *intuited in Christ* . . . He counts not as this *single* individual but as *universal* man, as true man . . . His *pain was the depth of unity of the divine and human nature in living suffering.*[5]

The doctrine of the Incarnation is, insists Hegel, "a certainty for humanity"—even the Trinitarian character of God reflects the logical structure of the dialectic. Hegel's theology interprets Jesus as the immanent incarnation of a truth that had been reached by consciousness, but not yet grasped conceptually.

Hegel's exposition of the dynamic, reciprocal relationship between the distinct aspects of being is formalized in his dialectical method. This breaks decisively with Aristotelian logic—which persists through Kant's philosophy—insofar as the old principle of contradiction becomes an occasion for reconciliation as well as a differentiating force. Hegel criticizes Kant for failing to recognize that the "antinomies of being," far from designating the limits of knowledge, direct our attention to the dialectical movement of thought. The real significance of the antinomies, argues Hegel, is that "everything actual contains opposed determinations within it," and that therefore "the comprehension of an object amounts precisely to our becoming conscious of it as a concrete unity of opposed determinations."[6] Whereas the Kantian understanding performs judgments that determine one appearance as 'A' and another as 'not-A,' according to Aristotelian laws of logic, for Hegel any particular thing is at once A and not-A, so that 'thinking it through' concretely involves traversing these opposites, and grasping the unity of the object by means of this movement.

Taking up the project of ontology that Hume and Kant had tried to lay to rest, Hegel, like Aristotle before him, addresses being as the manifest potency for movement and change. His philosophy, however, explores an historically aware plane of motion that is very different from the Greek cosmos, and this perspective allows Hegel to criticize Aristotelian logic as reflective of a relatively opaque form of consciousness. More simply, this means that Aristotle's logic is wrong, at least insofar as it claims to articulate eternal and immutable laws of thinking. Hegel argues that its principle of contradiction, which differentiates merely between 'A' and 'not-A,' relies on an abstract negativity, expressing a self-relation rather than a relation to a determinate other. He offers instead a concept of contradiction based on opposition or contrariness: any given term is contradicted by its opposite—for example, north and south. Here, it makes no difference which of the pair of opposites is called 'positive' and which 'negative,' for both terms apply equally to each. This is important because it brings difference *inside* the concept, at every level. Hegel challenges the law of the 'excluded middle' (any particular thing must be *either* A *or* not-A) that is implied by Aristotelian logic, arguing that two opposing terms are always related to one another by a unifying concept. Contradiction may express a difference, but this is grounded in identity: for example, north and south are both latitudinal direction, and their conceptual unity could be represented by drawing a straight, vertical line. Hegelian contradiction leads to a movement of unification, 'synthesis' or 'mediation.' Contradiction is the propelling force of the dialectic, "the moving principle of the world."[7]

Hegel's concept of contradiction as determinate opposition is central to his dynamic logic. The dialectical method proceeds by working through the simplest concepts and their opposites, in order to reach the more inclusive concept expressing their unity. This emerging, mediated concept then becomes the basis for further opposition to *its* 'other': "distinctions made are resolved as soon as they are made, and are made as soon as they are resolved, and what is true and actual is precisely this circular movement."[8] Beginning with "*being, pure being*, without any further determination," Hegel shows that this concept cannot be defined in distinction to anything outside it, because it signifies all that *is*. Because it has no specific content, the concept of being is an intuition of emptiness, or, equally, an empty intuition. But what is an empty intuition other than a pure act of intuiting? But then, what is a pure act of intuiting without an object? (Here we can see that in unfolding his definition of being, Hegel shifts from the passive to the active, from object to subject: an idea becomes an act of thinking, so that what starts off as an analytical account of the *content* of a concept leads to reflexive consideration of its *form*. This movement exemplifies the process of the dialectic from ideal to real, and then back to reflection upon this reality—the "mediated ideal.") Hegel concludes that pure being "is in fact nothing." The concept of nothing signifies the absence of all content and determination—and yet it does not disappear altogether: "nothing" certainly has a meaning, and, since meaning is the only kind of being an idea can claim to have, nothing *is* still *something*. As soon as this 'is,' without any further specification, is asserted, the thought of nothing becomes identical with the thought of being. This becoming-identical constitutes the dynamic relationship between two apparently opposing ideas:

> *Pure being* and *pure nothing* are, therefore, the same. What is the truth is neither being nor nothing, but that being—does not pass over but has passed over—into nothing, and nothing into being. But it is equally true that they are not undistinguished from each other, that, on the contrary, they are not the same, that they are absolutely distinct, and yet that they are unseparated and inseparable and that each immediately *vanishes into its opposite*. Their truth is, therefore, this movement of the immediate vanishing of the one into the other: *becoming*, a movement in which both are distinguished, but by a difference that has equally immediately resolved itself.[9]

In this rather beautiful passage Hegel unfolds the self-generating thought of becoming: we can see how logic itself reaches instability and transition as soon as meaning emerges. The 'synthesis' of being and nothing provided by 'becoming' is significant not because it somehow dissolves their opposition, but because it accomplishes the movement to a higher reflective level. Becoming expresses the comprehension of being and nothing, and of the relation between the two. There is a repeated movement whereby meaning is established, destabilized, and then relativized within a larger context. With this relativization emerges a wisdom, a recognition that whatever appears to be complete requires a deeper understanding—an understanding of the boundaries within which a mere moment seems like a totality. Worked out concretely, this dialectic produces a higher form of consciousness than the simple immediate idea; it is "consciousness raised to the second power" insofar as it is aware of itself and at the same time aware of its self-awareness.

Hegel's view that truth should be grasped as a process rather than as a static, eternally fixed idea means that becoming rises to even greater philosophical importance. It is, then, quite natural that Kierkegaard should have taken movement as the starting point for his account of human existence. However, having learned this much from Hegel, Kierkegaard turns all of his polemical energies against "the System," arguing that its movement remains confined to the sphere of ideality; that becoming involves a freedom that is incommensurable with the necessity of logic; and that "this impotence of logic is the transition to the sphere of becoming where existence and reality appear." Put another way, "only when reflection comes to a halt can a beginning be made."

Chapter Three

Kierkegaard's Critique of Hegel

Having considered how the philosophical question of movement has developed over the very broad historical period from Heraclitus to Hegel, we now shift our focus to the more immediate background to Kierkegaard's authorship. Kierkegaard was born in 1813—the year that Hegel's *Science of Logic* was published—and he spent the 1830s studying philosophy and theology at the University of Copenhagen. This decade within the academy was, of course, formative for Kierkegaard: Hegel's ideas were still fresh and exciting, and provoked fierce debates between his followers and his opponents. The preoccupation with movement that characterizes Hegelian philosophy prompted its detractors to turn with renewed interest to Aristotle, and to champion the old principle of contradiction in opposition to the dialectical logic of mediation. This intellectual milieu within which Kierkegaard served his philosophical apprenticeship provides invaluable insight into the theme of movement that emerges in the 1843 pseudonymous texts. However, during the 1830s Kierkegaard's development was influenced as much by his increasing dissatisfaction with academia as by his studies; questions of becoming took on a personal significance as he struggled to *exist* in an environment dominated by intellectual reflection.

This means that Kierkegaard's thematization of movement involves far more than evaluating the relative merits of Hegelian and Aristotelian accounts of becoming. This philosophical discussion does in fact take place in the 1843 texts, but it is dramatized within the theater of existence that is created through Kierkegaard's writing. His narrators and characters debate the principles of mediation and contradiction, discuss the ancient

Greek aporia of becoming, and question the limits of ethical reason—but they also experience melancholy, face decisions, and make journeys. One of the most striking aspects of Kierkegaard's renowned existentialism is his questioning of the academic, intellectual life *as an existential possibility*. Kierkegaard is responding primarily to Hegel, but also to philosophy in general, when he asks whether the truth and meaning of becoming can be communicated through concepts. Kierkegaard's interest in movement has to be understood in the context of his critique of Hegel, but because this critique is motivated by personal concerns as well as by philosophical *and* theological conflict, it requires very careful handling.

The philosophical positions and styles of Hegel and Kierkegaard are, at least in some respects, so profoundly antithetical that it can be difficult to make sense of their opposition without taking sides. Do we have to make a choice between *either* Hegel *or* Kierkegaard—between immanence and transcendence, reason and passion, world history and subjective existence? Do we have to decide that one thinker is right, and the other wrong? This possibility raises its own questions as to how such a judgment could be made, and what it might mean, with respect to philosophical positions. The problem is deepened further by the fact that opposition, or contradiction, is itself an issue that divides the two thinkers: the view that they are incommensurable is in a sense already Kierkegaardian, while any attempt to reconcile the two philosophies would incline toward an Hegelian standpoint. Kierkegaard opposes "the single individual" to the rational, systematic method, and in particular to the concept of mediation, with which he identifies Hegel; whereas the totalizing, historicizing force of Hegel's philosophy suggests that Kierkegaard's position, like all others, can be incorporated into the dialectic (perhaps at the stage of alienated, unhappy consciousness) as a 'moment' of the Idea's progressive self-comprehension.

In addition, the fact that Kierkegaard addresses Hegel polemically, rather than engaging directly with his texts, brings into question his understanding of Hegelian philosophy. Readers more sympathetic to Hegel might simply dismiss Kierkegaard's challenge as dogmatic and reactionary, and as an attack on a straw man. We must certainly bear in mind that Kierkegaard's encounter with Hegelian philosophy was mediated by the interpretations of speculative thinking that were circulating in the University of Copenhagen, and we will shortly examine these in some detail. It is true that much of Kierkegaard's acquaintance with Hegel was, at best, second hand: in 1837 he attended some of Martensen's lectures on Hegel's logic, but became bored by the second half of the course and resorted to copying the lecture notes from other students. During his stay in Berlin in 1841 Kierkegaard heard lectures on Hegelian philosophy and theology by Karl Werder, Philip Marheineke, and Schelling—but we do not know how much he read of Hegel's own work.

An instinctual antipathy to Hegelian ideas may have made Kierkegaard inclined to assimilate 'Hegel' as a philosophical phenomenon to the cruder speculative thought of certain Hegelians who lacked their mentor's insight and subtlety. However, we should not on this account dismiss Kierkegaard's criticisms, for his probable lack of scholarship is balanced by his brilliant (if quirky) intellect. Whether or not he was familiar with the details of Hegel's system, Kierkegaard's writing engages profoundly with the project of philosophy itself, and contains rare insight into its relevance for the existing individual.

Although the question of whether Kierkegaard is right about the inadequacies of Hegelian thought should not be ignored altogether, focusing on this provides a rather limiting basis for an exploration of his relationship to Hegel. We must remain aware that what emerges from Kierkegaard's pseudonymous writing is not a rigorous engagement with Hegel's texts, but a *dramatized* conflict between the perspectives of speculative philosophy and subjective individuality. For this reason, reading Kierkegaard with a view to producing a critical analysis of his objections to Hegel may obscure rather than illuminate his thought. Instead, we shall allow the caricature that represents Hegel and his philosophy to emerge as fully as possible, and then stay with—or rather, move with—this character as we pursue him through Kierkegaard's texts. In this way, the thematic and philosophical coherence of each text may be appreciated undisturbed, for the time being, by questions of comparative analysis.

The idea of a dramatic conflict between 'the single individual' and 'Hegel' will provide an important interpretative key as, in part 2, we examine each of Kierkegaard's 1843 texts in turn. In these commentaries, 'Hegel' refers primarily to Kierkegaard's literary reconstruction of speculative philosophy; the resemblances or disparities between this and Hegel's own writing should remain a distinct question—and one which we may be able to address with more clarity by the end of this book. For now, the most important question concerns the reasons for Kierkegaard's passionate opposition to Hegel above all other thinkers, and this cannot be answered simply by comparing one philosophy to the other. Allowing our interpretation of Kierkegaard's relationship to Hegel to be guided by the theme of movement will shed light on many of the difficulties that arise when we try to place these two thinkers side by side. It is also helpful at this stage to distinguish between the existential and intellectual aspects of this relationship, and to examine each in turn, in order to appreciate how both are interwoven in the pseudonymous texts.

∞

During the 1830s Kierkegaard, as a student, was in the phase of life caught between youth and maturity. These years represent a kind of intellectual and spiritual adolescence: a period of transition to the freedom and independence of adulthood, but also a time of instability, powerlessness, and perhaps above all conflict, both internal and external. This idea of adolescence provides a motif, a metaphor, for our interpretation of Kierkegaard's response to 'Hegel' as a literary (or 'aesthetic') construction, for it gathers several aspects of a complex relationship without forcing a systematic, logically consistent account—such accounts tending to confuse things further in the case of a writer such as Kierkegaard.

Regarding Kierkegaard's attack on Hegel as analogous to an adolescent's rebellion against his father helps us to understand how Kierkegaard was deeply influenced by Hegel while expressing intense hostility toward him. Underlying this hostility is a tone of disillusionment and disappointment: the sense that Hegel does not deliver what he promises—in, for example, his impressive preface to the *Phenomenology of Spirit*. Here, Hegel promises *movement*, but in Kierkegaard's view he "has willed something great, though without having achieved it." Johannes Climacus, who shares many features with Kierkegaard as a student, suggests that his struggles with Hegel's system are rooted in "having persuaded myself to think that it really meant something—instead of being merely loose thinking concealed behind pretentious expressions," and says that Hegel has "dealt indefensibly with an enthusiastic youth who believed him."[1]

Hegel's philosophy represents for Kierkegaard the standpoint of maturity (an authoritative, *absolute* standpoint) not only insofar as it is the work of an established professor, written in a very serious, grown-up style, but also in its implicit claim to express the culmination of conceptual understanding. This kind of philosophical reflection was an activity at which Kierkegaard himself excelled; more than this, he regarded it as essential to his character. In contrast to the polemic against speculative thought that we find in Kierkegaard's published writing, his journals record his "enigmatic respect for Hegel":

> I have learned much from him, and I know very well that I can still learn much more from him . . . His philosophical knowledge, his amazing learn-

ing, the insight of his genius, and everything else good that can be said of a philosopher I am willing to acknowledge and admire as any disciple.[2]

This praise implies, however, a certain reservation about the merits of philosophical thought itself—and Kierkegaard was extremely ambivalent toward his own outstanding intellectual powers. He relied upon his philosophical perspicuity and literary talent for his public status and success, and upon his incisive wit to defend himself from the mockery and criticism of others. But in his intensely reflective self-consciousness he knew that intellectuality was the very essence of his being—in his blood, as it were—and he questioned it deeply. Recalling his childhood in *The Point of View for My Work as an Author*, he states that "I began at once with reflection . . . I am reflection, from first to last." In his journal of 1838 he describes a "great earthquake" of his youth in which he was overcome by self-doubt:

> Then I suspected . . . that the outstanding intellectual gifts of our family were only given us in order that we should rend each other to pieces: then I felt the stillness of death grow around me when I saw my father, an unhappy man who was to outlive us all, a cross on the tomb of all his hopes.[3]

Beneath the brittle arrogance of Kierkegaard's intellectuality there is sadness and a sense of helplessness. He viewed reflection as at once a destructive force and a place of refuge: "in desperate despair I grasped at nothing but the intellectual side in man and clung fast to it, so that the thought of my own considerable powers of mind was my only consolation, ideas my one joy, and mankind indifferent to me." (As we shall see in the following chapter on *Either/Or*, the melancholy and indifference described here are defining features of the aesthetic personality.)

Kierkegaard's depression continued through his student years, and his "absolute spiritual incapacity"—together, perhaps, with a natural propensity for idleness—was reflected in his failure to apply himself to his studies. Several times he delayed sitting his theological examinations, and in 1839 he described the current phase of his life as "the longest parenthesis I have known." The following journal entry captures the mood that recurred throughout this time: "I live and feel these days somewhat as a chessman must feel when the opponent says: that piece cannot be moved—like a useless spectator, for my time is not yet come."[4] If movement signifies an individual's power of existing, then this metaphor of stasis expresses spiritual impotence. This sense of incapacity is borne out by an observation made in the summer of 1838 by Goldschmidt, the editor of the *Corsair*, who at the time was quite friendly with Kierkegaard. Goldschmidt describes how, as they were walking along together one day,

Kierkegaard made a strange, sudden leaping movement that seemed to be somehow inhibited:

> There was something sprightly about it, but it was altogether different from the sprightliness one sees elsewhere in the world. The movement was peculiar and almost painful to me . . . It was as if this learned, slender man wanted to enter into the joy of life, but either could not or must not.[5]

Kierkegaard repeatedly complained about the impotence and stasis of his life while he was at university: "this dreadful still life, so miserable and thin a life . . . Sadly my life is all too much in the subjunctive mood. Would to God I had some indicative power!"

Expressions of an inability to move are echoed by the young aesthete of *Either/Or*. In this text we find again the adolescent persona: the young man lacking direction, who is admonished by the mature, authoritative figure of Judge William. Kierkegaard's reflections on the stasis of melancholy, both in his personal writings and through the character of the aesthete, give us some indication of the psychological significance of the question of motion. This helps to illuminate Kierkegaard's critique of Hegel—and we shall explore it further in the following chapter—for what is particularly striking in *Either/Or* is Judge William's recognition of the *similarities* between the aesthete's attitude to life and the Hegelian principle of mediation: "at this point you are united with the philosophers. What unites you is that life comes to a stop."

In this way, the motif of adolescence functions to *identify* Hegelian philosophy as well as to characterize Kierkegaard's furious attack upon it. Kierkegaard's accusations against Hegel—of hypocrisy, arrogance, irresponsibility, misguidedness—call to mind the reproaches of an adolescent son. However, his rebellion against the existential possibility represented by Hegel—that of the abstract thinker, the academic philosopher—also casts Hegel in the adolescent role. From an existential point of view, Kierkegaard claims, intellectual reflection has not yet reached the seriousness of ethics. This means that *Either/Or*'s aesthete is an ambiguous character: on the one hand his melancholy and his lack of "indicative power" echo Kierkegaard's personal experiences as a student, and on the other hand his attitude of indifference resembles Hegelian philosophy. After leaving university—finally—in 1841, Kierkegaard remains aware that abstract thinking is a "temptation" for him, but he pushes his literary personae toward an ethical view of life that acknowledges the responsibilities of freedom, the significance of action.

And from this ethical perspective—represented most notably by Judge William—flows criticism of Hegelian philosophy and dissatisfaction with its categories. If Kierkegaard's published works, from *Either/Or* onward, represent his mature, independent philosophical position after finishing his academic training, they also attempt a more existential progression from a form of consciousness immersed in intellectual reflection.

Kierkegaard's personal struggle to *exist* within academic life helps to explain why, despite his considerable intellectual interests and abilities, he expresses such anti-intellectualism. Several years later he was able to take a more balanced view of abstract thought, condemning not reflection itself but "a standstill in reflection" as "the fraud and the corruption" of existence.[6] For Kierkegaard, Hegel's philosophy represents precisely this standstill in reflection (a kind of arrested adolescence), as does academic life generally. Although Hegel is often named as his target, he also speaks disparagingly of "university professors" and "privatdocents" when he is clearly referring to Hegelian ideas. In the *Postscript* the abstract thinker is depicted as a "pitiful professorial figure . . . whose personal life was devoid of pathos or struggles, concerned only with the question of which university offered the best livelihood." (A cynic might want to argue here that this is an easy position for Kierkegaard to assume, for he lived all his life on money provided by his father, who was a successful businessman, and that a 'spiritual' detachment from worldly affairs is much easier to bear when one has a substantial inheritance.) As we shall see in part 2, Kierkegaard argues that intellectuals—at least, those who take themselves too seriously—do not progress existentially beyond the aesthetic sphere to ethical maturity. In the light of this, Kierkegaard ridicules the Hegelian attempt to include accounts of ethics and religion *within* a philosophical system, and to claim for philosophers the highest spiritual task.

∞

Although Kierkegaard's opposition to Hegel was motivated in part by his personal disenchantment with the academic way of life and mode of discourse, he nevertheless gained from the academy the philosophical tools that enabled him to attack the Hegelian system. As I have suggested, the Hegel to whom Kierkegaard responds is, to a great extent, a personification of the speculative philosophy that was taught and debated at the University of Copenhagen during the 1830s. This decade was dominated by Hegelianism, insofar as the new philosophy was presented by its enthusiastic converts as a decisive challenge to the intellectual establishment, which therefore had to consolidate itself in opposition to Hegelian ideas. Aristotle became central to these debates, because the dialectical logic that is the starting point of Hegel's philosophy of mediation develops by breaking away from the rules of thought established by Aristotle. Hegelians praised the dialectical method as a genuine progression from classical logic; those who rejected all or part of the speculative philosophy were concerned to defend Aristotelian principles against its claims. So if we find in Kierkegaard's writing that the theme of movement is sometimes developed in terms of a confrontation between Aristotle's concept of kinesis and Hegel's concept of mediation, then this should be understood in the context of debates that were already taking place in Copenhagen during the decade prior to the first pseudonymous publications.[7]

Hegel attempts to construct a philosophical thinking that moves as consciousness moves; he suggests that concepts, and the consciousness in which they are embedded, reciprocally develop and unfold themselves. In his philosophy the logical laws that had previously been regarded as immutable, and necessarily so, are now historicized, relativized, and set into motion. The role of the immutable, the constant, is taken over by a dialectical principle of becoming that is itself primary, no longer in need of a distinct logical ground to make it intelligible. Whether Hegel was either justified or successful in creating this philosophy of mediation became the subject of much discussion in Prussian intellectual life. Herbart's *De principio logico exclusi medii inter contradictoria non negligendo commentatio* (1833) and Trendelenburg's *Logische Untersuchungen* (1840) both criticize Hegel's rejection of Aristotelian logic, focusing particularly on the issue of contradiction. Trendelenburg explicitly opposes Hegel's attempt to introduce movement into logic—and when Kierkegaard came across his work in 1844 he was delighted to find a kindred spirit whose knowledge of Aristotle was far deeper and more rigorous than his own.[8]

The debates surrounding classical and dialectical logic were taken up in Copenhagen, where the most influential proponents of Hegelian philosophy were Johan Heiberg and Hans Martensen. Heiberg, a poet and dramatist, was initially drawn to Hegel's lectures on aesthetics, but he became enthusiastic about all aspects of speculative philosophy. In the early 1830s Heiberg delivered and published lectures on Hegelian logic, and in 1837 he began a journal called *Perseus, Journal for the Speculative Idea*, in which he published "The System of Logic," an article offering an introduction to a complete Hegelian aesthetics. As an ambitious young writer, Kierkegaard was naturally attentive to Heiberg's literary activities: while he was a student he wrote a few short articles for *Copenhagen's Flying Post*, also edited by Heiberg, and he hoped that his *From the Papers of One Still Living* would be published in *Perseus*. Kierkegaard's subsequent disillusionment with Heiberg is apparent when, several years later, he ridicules "The System of Logic," "which, despite all movement, does not come further than to paragraph 23 . . . and despite its proud title, was not able to emancipate itself from a very subordinate existence in a flimsy periodical."[9] Heiberg's journal is important for us, however, insofar as it initiated the Danish debates about Hegel and Aristotle that were to influence Kierkegaard's authorship. For example, F. C. Sibburn, who was Kierkegaard's dissertation supervisor, published in 1838 a critical review of *Perseus*, "On the Manner in which the Law of Contradiction Is Treated in the Hegelian School," which opposed the theory of mediation and defended Aristotle's logic.

This academic debate concerning the principles of contradiction and mediation becomes particularly significant from our perspective when it turns to the theological and religious implications of the two systems of logic. Hegelian logic is not intended merely as a theoretical grounding for higher philosophical tasks: rather, the dialectical pattern is repeatedly reflected through diverse ontological spheres, from the dynamics of world history to the three-fold essence of God. For Hegel, logic marks the beginning of philosophy rather than its foundation. So whereas medieval and early modern theologians could either use classical, Aristotelian logic in the service of Christian dogmatics, or posit an absolute disjunction between conceptual thought and a mystical relationship to God, Hegel's dialectical logic is presented as the structure of the real, the actual, and thus as inseparable from concrete existence. This new philosophy inspired people to think of truth as a shape, form, or structure that changes through time; to understand human thought in terms of the developing shapes of collective consciousness; and to seek the coherence of the Absolute Idea among the totality of ideas.

Hans Martensen was the most prominent Hegelian theologian in Denmark during the 1830s. He was a close friend of Heiberg, and he also taught Hegel's philosophy to students in Copenhagen. In 1839 one of these students, a theology graduate called Bornemann, unwittingly initiated a fierce debate when he published a sympathetic review of Martensen's dissertation *On the Autonomy of Human Self-Consciousness*. In his article Bornemann made the rather off-hand comment that "in theology both rationalism and supernaturalism are antiquated standpoints which belong to a time that has disappeared," implying an Hegelian overcoming of the opposition between these two modes of religious belief. This provoked Bishop Mynster, one of Denmark's most well-respected theologians, to respond publicly to this sort of Hegelian interpretation of religion—which was becoming increasingly popular. Mynster's article, "Rationalism, Supernaturalism," argued that these positions must be clarified as meaningfully distinct from one another; as both flourishing within contemporary theological debate; and as providing real alternatives to the Christian believer. In focusing on these religious issues, Mynster deepened the debate by offering a perspective on Hegelian thought that was not grounded solely on philosophical concerns. He concluded his article by appealing to Aristotle's law of the 'excluded middle' in support of his claim that rationalism and supernaturalism really are contradictory beliefs.

Heiberg then retaliated with an article that addressed Sibbern's criticisms of Hegelian philosophy as well as the arguments put forward by Bishop Mynster. This was followed by another article by Martensen, who supported Heiberg's defense of Hegel but, as a theologian, focused more particularly on the implications of mediation for Christian doctrine. Martensen's article, "Rationalism, Supernaturalism and the *principium exclusi medii*," suggests that the contrast between Judaism and Christianity is essentially the same as the contrast between Aristotelian and Hegelian logic. These two religions express different forms of truth, for each reflects a different consciousness of God: while Jewish faith is characterized by a radical, irreconcilable division between human beings and a transcendent God, the Christian incarnation offers mediation. Martensen argues that Judaism, in rejecting Jesus as the Son of God, rests on the Aristotelian assumption "that the contradictory predicates 'God' and 'man' could not be mediated in the self-same subject." The doctrine of the incarnation, on the other hand, "shows precisely that Christian metaphysics cannot remain in an either/or, but that it must find its truth in the third which [the law of the excluded middle] excludes."[10] In this way Hegelian mediation marks a progression in man's spiritual understanding, enabling thought to reach heights of truth and depths of meaning that could not be adequately grasped within the laws of Aristotelian logic. Martensen goes on to emphasize the immanence of Christianity, in contrast to Jewish transcendence: through the incarnation God enters the human world, and the task of modern theology is to understand this concept of an immanent God.

> The immanent thinking inspired by the dialectic . . . does not find any rest before it knows the [divine] mystery as revelation. If the Trinity is really to have meaning for thought, as the absolute truth, then it must also claim that this meaning becomes the key to the entire system of the world, then all actuality in heaven and on earth must be taken up

into its circle, then it must be known as the concept that conceives itself and everything.[11]

We can recognize here the kind of Hegelian vocabulary that Kierkegaard reacts to so strongly: the notion of the "absolute truth" of Christianity, and of its place within the "entire system of the world"; insistence on its immanence and its accessibility to conceptual thought. We can also see a connection between Kierkegaard's *Either/Or* and this debate about Aristotelian and Hegelian logic. In his article Martensen several times uses the expression "aut/aut," and its Danish equivalent "enter/eller," to characterize Mynster's insistence on an absolute dichotomy between rationalism and supernaturalism—"Is it not the task of our age to sublate this disastrous aut/aut?" It was, then, quite natural for Kierkegaard to seize on the phrase "either/or" as the title of his indirect polemic against Hegelian mediation.

∞

In 1842 Bishop Mynster stepped back into the debate, using a review of publications by Herbart and Fichte on the laws of Aristotelian logic to respond to Martensen's Hegelian theology. This article is both better researched and more philosophical than his previous paper on rationalism and supernaturalism, and in the present context it is the most interesting contribution to the debate. Mynster, like Kierkegaard, was drawn into the discussion about mediation primarily because of its implications for Christianity, but unlike Kierkegaard he responds to Hegelian ideas by focusing mostly on theological doctrine. He is concerned to clarify those beliefs which must—and those which must not—be associated with true Christianity, whereas Kierkegaard tends to leave these questions alone and to concentrate on the subjective, existential requirements of religious faith. But Mynster's insistence on an either/or in matters of doctrine does provide a positive ground for the possibility of ethical choice, which is essential to Kierkegaard's "task of becoming a Christian." In addition, they share a conviction that belief in God's transcendence is indispensable, and must be defended against any aspects of Hegelian thought that threaten to undermine it.

Mynster's strategy in criticizing the principle of mediation is to delimit the scope of its application. He argues that mediation occurs within the realm of empirical things, which are constantly subject to change. In the sphere of concepts, however—where, for Hegel, mediation is exemplified most clearly—Mynster insists that Aristotle's rules of logic are unshakeable, for the function of concepts is to determine, and thus give meaning to, the flux of empirical data. Categorizing opposing positions such as rationalism and supernaturalism, and theism and atheism, as concepts, he argues that in the interests of clarity their distinction from one another must be emphasized. These theological concepts, Mynster claims, "designate an actual and irresolvable contradiction."[12]

At first glance this argument may not bear much resemblance to Kierkegaard's critique of Hegel, for Mynster seems to be suggesting that religious beliefs are conceptual. However, this view leads him to recognize that rationalism and supernaturalism, and—perhaps more importantly—theism and atheism, really are contradictory positions. And this means that the existing individual has to choose between them, to affirm one by excluding the other. The decision between accepting and rejecting belief in God is a question of either/or:

> The completely contradictory opposite of theism is atheism; of this pantheism can be the most acceptable subspecies. But it must deny itself, must become another teaching, if it is to become theistic . . . Supernaturalism must always have rationalism outside itself, not in itself, and vice versa . . . in respect to the characteristic thing in both points of view, by which they have received their names in the language, the law of exclusion is valid; aut/aut: there is no third.[13]

Mynster does not say that this choice of "aut/aut" is itself conceptual or rational. Each position may be expressed conceptually, but this does not imply that the contradictory pair share a common rational ground upon which a decision could be made. As for Martensen's view that the principle of mediation can be applied to Christian doctrine, Mynster does see some truth in this. However, this sympathy is based not on enthusiasm for Hegelian ideas, but on quotations from the scriptures. Mynster's attitude to philosophy is that, although it can yield interesting and thought-provoking insights, Christianity does not need to seek philosophical support for the truths expressed in the Bible.

Like Kierkegaard, Mynster opposes the Hegelian attempt to conceive of Christianity immanently, as the full reconciliation of God and humanity. He argues instead that God's essence always has been, and always will be, simultaneously together with and apart from His creation. Central to Mynster's article is an attack on Martensen's attempt to distinguish between Judaism and Christianity on the basis of transcendence and immanence. Using references to the Old Testament, Mynster demonstrates that the Jewish God is by no means remote from the world: "Am I a God afar off, and not a God close at hand? Do I not fill heaven and earth?" (Jer. 23:23); "Whither shall I go from thy Spirit? Or whither shall I flee from thy presence? If I ascend to heaven, thou art there! If I make my bed in hell, thou art there! If I take the wings of the morning, and dwell in the uttermost parts of the sea, even there shall thy right hand lead me" (Psalm 139). Mynster argues that immanence is an indispensable aspect of Jewish and Christian religion, insofar as God is directly involved in the world and in human concerns. However, it is by virtue of their insistence on God's transcendence, on His elevation above and separation from the world, that both these religions are theistic.

Although Mynster engages seriously with the logical and philosophical issues integral to this debate, he concludes his article by explaining that his religious beliefs provide the foundation for his thinking. His comments express the view, shared by Kierkegaard, that philosophy does not provide the individual with the kind of truth within which he can exist. Mynster makes it clear that he finds such a home within Christianity, and not in any philosophical system. He presents philosophy and faith as two alternative perspectives, and rejects the Hegelian ambition to comprehend the whole of Spirit from an absolute position. As a Christian, he approaches God "from below," in a movement of "ascension":

> That I cannot go in for [my opponents'] point of view is not due to the fact that I am prejudiced or antiquated in now old-fashioned systems . . . For my part I must abandon the hope of being able to "look down from above"; but to those who feel the same lack of ability to do this as I do, I wish the same consolation which comforts me, that also from below one can see the highest, and when one also keeps it in mind, one ascends towards it.[14]

The implication is that Hegelian philosophy—or philosophers—cannot make this upward movement, because the speculative assumption of an omniscient perspective, *sub specie aeternis*, conceals the possibility of a personal, religious relationship to God. Kierkegaard would no doubt agree with this, although he also emphasizes that the abstract thinker, in trying to absorb all of existence into an act of reflection, looks away from himself. And as he was acutely aware, by attempting to "gain the world" in this way the individual is in danger of losing his own soul.

Part Two

Chapter Four

Either/Or: Kierkegaard's Principle of Contradiction

When Kierkegaard published *Either/Or* in March 1843, its title was already resonant with philosophical significance. As we have seen, the phrase "either/or" had been employed by Danish theologians such as Martensen and Mynster to denote the logical principle of contradiction, in the context of their debate about Hegelian mediation. This principle of contradiction was, we recall, established by Aristotle, and functions to anchor his account of kinesis as the movement from potentiality to actuality. In opposition to both Aristotle and Kant, Hegel argues that contradiction, rather than representing the limit of rational thought, provides the occasion for its own overcoming through mediation. By subsuming the diverse and perplexing contents of his first major work under the title *Either/Or*, Kierkegaard gives a preliminary indication of its opposition to Hegelian philosophy, and of its defense of a kind of movement which this philosophy threatens to undermine.

In *Either/Or* we find Kierkegaard's first attempt to articulate a plane of motion constituted by subjective, existential *inwardness*. In his preface, Victor Eremita raises the question of contradiction in relation to this idea of inwardness, suggesting that—contrary to Hegel's view that interiority is dialectically continuous with its external expression (or, in other words, that the internal and the external are moments of the process of mediation)—an individual's inward life may remain concealed:

> Dear Reader, I wonder if you may not sometimes have felt inclined to doubt a little the correctness of the philosophical maxim that the external is the internal, and the internal the external. Perhaps you have cherished in your heart a secret which you felt in all its joy or pain was too precious for you to share with another.

These opening sentences of *Either/Or* do not merely question the content of Hegel's "philosophical maxim": through an appeal to the subjective experience of the individual reader to whom they are addressed, they challenge the whole project of philosophical reflection. Knowledge, which is made possible by the transparency of concepts, is here opposed by the inner experience of secrecy—an experience that each reader must surely recognize as his own. As Kierkegaard later explains, *Either/Or* constitutes "a polemic against the truth as knowledge."[1]

This theme of secrecy dominates the preface (and recurs in the aesthete's writings, particularly in his discussion of Antigone). Victor Eremita suggests that the text he is introducing testifies to his belief in a hidden inwardness—not only because he thinks that the inner personalities of its two authors contradict their outward appearances, but because the manuscript itself was for years concealed within an escritoire, behind a secret door. In his preface, Kierkegaard's pseudonym invokes instances of contradiction between inner truth and external manifestation in order to challenge Hegel's description of spiritual progress in terms of increasing self-transparency. Ultimately, this strategy aims to protect and to preserve the interiority of Kierkegaard's plane of motion, and its subjective freedom, from the rationalizing necessity of mediation. When Johannes Climacus reviews *Either/Or* in the *Postscript*, he prioritizes this aspect of its opposition to speculative philosophy: "If [this book] has any merit, this will essentially consist in not giving any result, but in transforming everything into inwardness."

This transformation into inwardness is precisely the movement of becoming ethical that is described in the second volume of *Either/Or*, and it reaches its greatest intensity in the sermon at the end of the book, which presents the possibility of a religious consciousness. The becoming-inward of the existing individual is a movement not only because it involves a "transformation," a qualitative change, but also insofar as *inwardness is itself dynamic*, a free power of self-actualization. The transition from an aesthetic personality to existential inwardness is a transition from spiritual stasis to spiritual movement.

So, it seems that if we pay attention to the way in which Kierkegaard handles the issue of contradiction, we can learn something about his idea of inwardness. One of the first things we learn, however, is that inwardness is opposed to Hegelian mediation—opposed, that is, to a movement that takes place in the medium of ideality. Inwardness cannot be truly spoken of as an idea; rather, it signifies an *existential* kind of movement. Kierkegaard offers this movement—soon to be explicitly formulated as repetition—in place of mediation. In *Either/Or*, existential movement is not given a name, but it is expressed thematically throughout the writings of both the aesthete and Judge William. Between these characters Kierkegaard unfolds the issue of contradiction: the question of either/or. This question is repeated in the "Ultimatum," where it is directly addressed to the reader (who is ordered to "read this and think of yourself"); where it becomes concerned with the individual's relationship to God; and where it concludes with a pronouncement on the nature of truth. In posing these questions in connection with either/or, Kierkegaard raises the stakes in the contemporary debate about mediation as he offers his own account of movement and contradiction.

∞

The debates in Copenhagen during the 1830s concerning Hegelian and Aristotelian logic provide an illuminating context for *Either/Or*. As we have seen, Bishop Mynster repeats Aristotle's insistence on the principle of contradiction in order to emphasize, in opposition to Hegelian mediation, the requirement to choose between two irreducibly distinct alternatives. More specifically, he argues that from the perspective of the existing individual—as opposed to that of speculative philosophy—acceptance and rejection of Christian doctrine constitute an either/or.

Kierkegaard's either/or also functions to distinguish two forms of existence: the aesthetic, exemplified by the nameless author of volume one, and the ethical, exemplified by Judge William. For Kierkegaard, however, this distinction is not merely external: his either/or means more than the obvious question of *either* the aesthetic *or* the ethical. Either/or, *as principle of contradiction*, distinguishes the two perspectives *internally* insofar as it is significantly lacking from the aesthetic attitude, while being predominant within the ethical. The principle of contradiction—as Mynster had already recognized—indicates a choice, a decision, an acceptance of freedom; and Kierkegaard suggests that the absence of this contradiction is the source of the inadequacy of aesthetic existence. The aesthete is *indifferent* to the choices available to him, and so he is *incapable* of making a meaningful choice between them. This incapacity amounts to a lack of freedom, an impotence to bring about the existential movement of becoming the self one has chosen to be. Judge William, by contrast, champions self-choice—which, in his own case, is manifested in his commitment to marriage—and urges the aesthete to face his freedom.

Implicit in *Either/Or* is the idea that the inadequacies of the aesthetic life—encapsulated by its denial of contradiction—are characteristic of Hegelian philosophy too. Indeed, this assimilation of Hegelian thought and aesthetic existence runs through each of the 1843 pseudonymous texts; Kierkegaard's critique of Hegel is often enclosed within his portrayal of the aesthetic. (For example, when he discusses *Either/Or* in the *Postscript*, Climacus's descriptions of Hegelian philosophy and of the aesthete are interchangeable: speculative thought "is indifferent to the existential," while the aesthete "has thought everything possible, and yet he has not existed at all.") Here, it is the principle of contradiction, or rather its negation, that functions as the main source of this assimilation—hence the title *Either/Or*.

Kierkegaard's basic contention is that Hegelian philosophy, despite its pretensions to include ethics and religion within its system, is confined within an aesthetic perspective that can realize neither. The aesthetic consciousness is powerless to make the movements that constitute ethical and religious existence, because these movements first require a commitment to the principle of either/or. This illuminates Judge William's remark that the aesthete's attitude

> bears a strange resemblance to the pet theory of the newer philosophy, that the principle of contradiction is annulled . . . You mediate contradictions in a higher madness, philosophy mediates them in a higher unity . . . At this point you are united with the philosophers. What unites you is that life comes to a stop.[2]

Kierkegaard's idea of a movement that depends on contradiction recalls Aristotle's account of kinesis. If Kierkegaard argues, like Aristotle, that real movement requires the principle of contradiction, what is the form of this 'requirement'? For Aristotle, contradiction is a rule of logic and secures the intelligibility of his concept of kinesis. For Kierkegaard, on the other hand, the principle of contradiction signifies the either/or of existential choice, which gives the subjective movement of decision real significance. These two accounts of movement are clearly positioned very differently: there is nothing logical about the way Kierkegaard's principle of contradiction 'grounds' the individual's self-actualization. However,

Either/Or: Kierkegaard's Principle of Contradiction 53

there is for both thinkers an essential connection between either/or and the actuality of motion.

Locating *Either/Or* within the context of the Danish debate about mediation and contradiction gives us insight into Kierkegaard's thought at a time when it was still being crystallized, and brings out dimensions of the text that tend to be overlooked by commentators. However, another accomplishment of reading *Either/Or* as responsive to this debate is to highlight Kierkegaard's distance from it, and from the whole intellectual milieu within which it arose. This clarifies the significance of the existential sphere that he attempts to penetrate—and perhaps even to establish—through his writing. In *Either/Or*, Kierkegaard is seeking a place, a position, which is quite different from that occupied by professional, academic philosophers, and indeed this distinction is itself one of the essential movements of his authorship.

Because Kierkegaard wants to place philosophical reflection—which, in its flights of abstraction, he believes to be epitomized by the Hegelian system—within his category of the aesthetic, any existential movement beyond this category demands a departure from philosophy. As a contribution to the debate concerning contradiction and mediation, *Either/Or* not only reflects on but actualizes this movement: the text attempts to transcend the academic debate through the new perspective that it brings to its questions. Instead of stepping into the discussion by publishing another article in an academic journal, Kierkegaard *dramatizes* the argument through the characters of the aesthete and Judge William. In *Either/Or* the academic debate is aestheticized, just as philosophy itself is relegated to the aesthetic sphere—to the lowest position within Kierkegaard's existential schema. Of course, Kierkegaard cannot resist the temptation to philosophize: all four of the text's main voices provide opportunities for philosophical reflection, as well as expressing explicit or implicit criticism of this reflection as a mode of existence.

In *Either/Or*, then, the movement that is at stake in the debate about mediation and contradiction becomes a theme that functions to distinguish the aesthetic and ethical approaches to life. The two volumes of the text offer two existential possibilities: the first characterized by the indifference of mediation, and the second by the decisiveness implied by contradiction. Through their juxtaposition, and through the critique of the first expressed by the second, Kierkegaard presents an opposition conditioned by denial or acceptance of the principle of contradiction. The indifference, impotence, melancholy, and preoccupation with the past exhibited by the aesthete's reflections are described in terms of *stasis*, whereas Judge William's letters proclaim responsibility, freedom, purpose, awareness of the future, and *movement*.

∽

The aesthete's writings function as an indirect critique of Hegelian philosophy, by means of the resemblance between them. Both are characterized by a rejection of the principle of contradiction, and this rejection, Kierkegaard argues, is linked to a lack of movement. This connection between contradiction and movement is preserved from Aristotle's philosophy—but Kierkegaard is, of course, concerned with a different kind of movement and a different kind of contradiction. In order to understand the implications of the equivalence he finds between the aesthete and Hegelian philosophy, we need to look more closely at the significance that the concepts of motion and contradiction attain when they are transferred to the plane of existential subjectivity (in the first place, they are no longer encountered *as concepts*).

Kierkegaard's either/or represents the fact of choice for a finite, existing individual. The simple point here is that at any particular moment in time a person can be here or there, speaking or silent, married or unmarried—*but he can never be both at once*. It is for this reason, which one might call the principle of contradiction, that choices have to be made at all, and indeed at all times. In *Repetition* this recurrence of the moment of freedom is presented as a new philosophical category, essential to a "modern" interpretation of human existence; here in *Either/Or* we can see how this category develops from the issue of contradiction.

The aesthete does not actually deny the choice represented by either/or, but he reduces it to insignificance through his attitude of indifference. This is most clearly expressed in his "ecstatic lecture" on either/or: "whether you marry or do not marry, you will regret both . . . whether you hang yourself or do not hang yourself, you will regret both." This indifference, by neutralizing the alternatives and so negating the choice between them, leads to a thoroughly nihilistic attitude—and the aesthete concludes that "my life is utterly meaningless." This suggests a parallel with the Hegelian principle of mediation, which, as Kierkegaard often remarks, proceeds through negation. The fragment of verse attached to the aesthete's "Diapsalmata" expresses the consequences of mediation when it is translated into an existential attitude:

> *Tout n'est que vent, que fumée:*
> *Pour mieux dire, tout n'est rien.*

This amounts to a denial of existence itself: the aesthete experiences his life as a dream, populated by "pale, bloodless, tenacious and nocturnal shapes," a realm of possibilities all equally lacking the power of actualization. (This sentiment is later echoed in *Two Ages*, where Kierkegaard argues that Hegel's relativization of the principle of contradiction denies "the passionate disjunction between subjectivity and objectivity," and "lacks full-blooded individuality.")

This brings us to another essential characteristic of the aesthetic form of life: its spiritual impotence. Aristotle's kinesis, we recall, involves a capacity, a potency for movement; it expresses the *power* that brings a new quality into existence. This power of becoming, of actualization, is precisely what the aesthete lacks: the best he can do is rotate his crops (an immanent movement). In his "Diapsalmata," the aesthete expresses his sense of incapacity and paralysis:

> Cornelius Nepos tells us of a certain commander, who was shut up in a fortress with a considerable force of cavalry, and who ordered the horses to be whipped every day, lest they be injured by too much standing still—so I live these days like one besieged.
>
> I feel the way a chessman must, when the opponent says of it, that piece cannot be moved.[3]

In the *Postscript*, again, Climacus remarks on the aesthete's "weakness in winning through to existence." The vocabulary of strength and weakness that Kierkegaard's characters use in their discussion of contradiction highlights the issue of freedom that is at stake here: in its existential sense, the either/or is connected to the individual's active power to make decisions. In *Two Ages* Kierkegaard argues, more explicitly than in *Either/Or*, that "the principle of contradiction *strengthens* the individual in faithfulness to himself," suggesting that a person is prompted to make up his mind by "the creative omnipotence implicit in the passion of absolute disjunction."[4]

Although *Either/Or*'s aesthete speaks of his paralysis as if it were imposed upon him by some external force, his confinement is of course internal, and he is only deceiving himself by looking outward for the source of his sorrow. This indicates that the aesthete—like the Hegelian dialectic—is governed by necessity: despite his freedom to move between possibilities, seeking out new forms of pleasure, he lacks the power to realize any of them. This becomes explicit when Judge William compares the aesthetic and the ethical forms of life:

> The aesthetic is that in a man whereby he immediately is the man he is; the ethical is that whereby a man becomes what he becomes. By this I do not intend to say that the man who lives aesthetically does not develop, but he develops by necessity, not by freedom, no metamorphosis takes place within him, no infinite movement whereby he becomes what he becomes.[5]

To say that no power occurs *within* the individual is to suggest that he lacks the capacity for self-movement that, for Aristotle, constitutes the nature of a living being.

Because the aesthetic consciousness, insofar as it is identified with Hegelian thought, is supposed to constitute an attack upon it, we have to raise the question of what is *wrong* with this view of life. One might, after all, argue that the aesthete's indifference and impotence merely reflect the truth of human existence: that life has no meaning and that the self has no power. The simple answer to our question, however, is that the aesthete is unhappy. His writings are pervaded by his melancholy mood; he *suffers* from the lack of purpose in his life. Indifference is not 'wrong' from the point of view of knowledge; as a conclusion arrived at by the understanding, it is not irrational or erroneous. On the contrary, it is absolutely rational—and it is precisely this confinement within rationality that Kierkegaard wants to condemn as existentially impotent and nihilistic.

The aesthete's indifference is the existential expression of the denial of contradiction; his impotence is the existential expression of the absence of movement. Indifference and impotence are united insofar as, for Kierkegaard, they both signify a lack of passion—that feature of consciousness that represents its interest in life, its affirmation of life's significance. Passion is an intensification within consciousness, a "movement on the spot" that constitutes its power of actualization. As we saw in chapter 1, in the *Postscript* Climacus suggests that passion is the existential correlate of Aristotle's "unmoved mover," which provides the ultimate source of motion in the cosmos. Like Aristotle's God, passion functions to anchor the flux and relativity of finite existence. Because the aesthete has no passion, his inner world resembles Heraclitus's *cosmos*: without any fixed points or solid ground, everything is true and so nothing is true; everything is in motion and no*thing* is in motion. Affirmation and negation become identical: "what am I good for?—for nothing or for everything," sighs the hopeless young man.

For Kierkegaard, passion signifies intensity, a 'fullness' of being that expresses the power of the individual's inwardness. By contrast, the aesthete's inner being is a vacuum: "life is so empty and meaningless . . . how barren is my soul . . . always before me an empty space." This emptiness is predicated of the future in particular: the aesthete's melancholy is linked both to an annihilation of the future—insofar as he lacks the power to propel himself forward, to actualize himself—and to a preoccupation with the past. This relationship to time is described as a kind of paralysis: "Time flows, life is a stream, people say, and so on. I do not notice it. Time stands still, and I with it."[6] Again, this distinction between past and future is crucial to Kierkegaard's critique of Hegelian thought: indeed, philosophical knowledge in general is identified with a backward movement of recollection, whereas subjective existence requires the forward movement of repetition. Corresponding to this is the opposition between necessity and freedom, for Hegel's logic of necessity applies after the fact—it mediates the past. If mediation did turn toward the future it would annihilate its openness by anticipating it as already determined—producing, as it were, a premature history, instead of grasping the freedom that the future represents.

The aesthete's unhappy fixation with the past is expressed through the theme of grief, which is one of his favorite topics for reflection. In "Shadowgraphs" he discusses the grief of various literary characters (all of them abandoned women), addressing this collection of short essays to the *Symparanekromenoi*, or "fellowship of buried lives." The purpose of this little club, says the aesthete, is to uncover "the secrets of sorrow." In his portrait of "The Unhappiest Man" he recalls the legend of Niobe, who is turned into stone through grief for her dead children—in other words, she is paralyzed by her relationship to the past: "No hope allures her, no future moves her, no prospect tempts her, no hope excites her—hopeless she stands, petrified in memory . . . the world changes, but she knows no change; and time flows on, but for her there is no future time."[7] No doubt the aesthete empathizes with Niobe's plight, for he too admits: "I can describe hope so vividly that every hoping individual will acknowledge my description; and yet it is a deception, for while I picture hope, I think of memory."[8]

Judge William, in his second letter to the aesthete, makes an explicit connection between this preoccupation with the past and the practice of philosophy. "Philosophy," he says, "turns towards the past." It is clear that he has in mind here Hegelian mediation: although Judge William speaks of philosophy in general, Hegel's emphasis on world history makes him Kierkegaard's principle target. In contrast to the view that certain forms of Christianity are "antiquated standpoints"—which, as we saw in the previous chapter, was popular among some Hegelians—the judge suggests that it is the philosopher who resembles "an antiquarian." He argues that philosophy, like the aesthete, is unable to cope with ethical questions concerning the future:

> The philosopher says, "That's the way it has been hitherto." I ask, "What am I to do if I do not want to become a philosopher?" For if I want to do that, I see clearly enough that I, like the other philosophers, shall soon get to the point of mediating the past . . . There is no answer to my question of what I ought to do; for if I was the most gifted philosophical mind that ever lived in the world, there must be one more thing I have to do besides sitting and contemplating the past.[9]

The question about what to do in the future, "if I do not want to become a philosopher," seems to belong more to Kierkegaard than to Judge William: while the latter is settled in his chosen life, Kierkegaard at this time was beginning his writing career, had recently fled from marriage, and was still uncertain about his vocation. He is perhaps delivering a warning to himself—a warning that may also be directed to ourselves, his readers. For, as we read and write about Kierkegaard today, what are we doing other than contemplating the past? Isn't there something *better* we have to do? (Maybe it is no wonder that intellectuals tend to be melancholic!) This is not the last time that Kierkegaard's antiphilosophical philosophy will force his readers into an uncomfortable, even paradoxical position.

∞

Movement is essential to *Either/Or*'s second volume—Judge William's ethical lecture to the aesthete—in at least two ways. First, the configuration of characteristics that define the aesthetic sphere, and that are articulated by metaphors of stasis, are opposed by a configuration expressed in terms of movement. In the judge's ethical view, indifference, impotence, necessity, melancholy, and a preoccupation with the past must be replaced by responsibility, decisiveness, freedom, purpose, and an interest in the future. All these possibilities, he argues, must be chosen in order to make the movements of one's life one's own. This demand of choice—the rallying cry of "either/or!"—leads to the second aspect of the significance of movement, for one *becomes* ethical through an act of choice. Some kind of transition occurs in becoming ethical; something new is actualized, brought into being; an existential kinesis takes place. And it is precisely this movement that Kierkegaard launches against Hegelian philosophy and its progressive dialectic—an opposition personified by the aesthete and Judge William. Reviewing *Either/Or* in the *Postscript*, Climacus tells us that the relation between the aesthetic and the ethical "is not to be conceived as that between an immature and a mature thought, but between existing and not existing." This means that becoming ethical involves what Aristotle would have called "a coming-into-existence kind of change," a transition from non-being to being.

The pivotal point of Judge William's account of the ethical is the act of choice. In order to become ethical, the aesthete has to fulfill his capability—his power, his freedom, his dunamis—to make decisions. Instead of negating the value of the alternatives available to him through his attitude of indifference, the aesthete must affirm the significance of his choice by— by what? Simply, it seems, by choosing. (The idea that choice itself is an active, actualizing power is illustrated by Kierkegaard's response when his servant Westergaard asked him about the immortality of the soul. Westergaard hoped that his employer would, as a learned man, be able to provide some assurance of this, but Kierkegaard only replied "that we are all equally ignorant on such points; that one had to choose between the one possibility and the other; and that conviction then comes in accordance with the choice.")[10] This subjective process of actualization, like its objective version as kinesis, needs to recognize the principle of contradiction, and thus Judge William makes his own contribution to the philosophical debate about contradiction and mediation.

In his "ecstatic lecture" on either/or, the aesthete finds that the principle of contradiction expresses indifference and, consequently, nihilism. Judge William, by contrast, declares that "that which is prominent in my either/or is the ethical . . . It is a question of the reality of the act of choice."[11] Again, there is here a parallel to the function of contradiction in the concept of kinesis: just as Aristotle's logical principle secures his account of the reality of motion, so Judge William's either/or secures "the reality of the act of choice." This act of choice is integral to motions on the plane of subjective individuality. Like other Danish intellectuals such as Mynster and Sibbern (although, of course, in a manner very *unlike* theirs), Kierkegaard invokes this either/or against Hegelian mediation.

In his challenge to speculative philosophy, one of the points of contention that Kierkegaard emphasizes most strongly is that of necessity and freedom. As we have seen, Judge William criticizes the aesthete because "no movement takes place within him": he is not the free source of his movements; he is impotent to actualize himself. The crux of this problem, argues the judge, is the issue of contradiction:

> If we concede mediation, then there is no absolute choice . . . then there is no absolute either/or. This is the difficulty, yet I believe that it

is due partly to the fact that two spheres are confounded with one another: that of thought and that of freedom. The opposition does not subsist for thought, which goes over to the other side and thereupon combines both in a higher unity. For freedom the opposition does subsist, for freedom excludes the other side.[12]

Here, Judge William—again rather like Bishop Mynster—advances his argument by establishing the distinct 'spheres' within which the principles of mediation and contradiction have their validity. (This clear distinction between thought and freedom is itself in opposition to the Hegelian method, which seeks to permeate everything with the Idea.) These spheres are, for Kierkegaard, existential rather than logical or metaphysical: they signify different forms of consciousness. The aesthetic consciousness is characterized by necessity, by stasis, and it *becomes ethical* by transforming itself through the moment of decision. This is a movement inward, a movement of intensification; consciousness consolidates itself in its act of choice, "transforms a merely outward life and gives it inwardness."[13] Every choice is an act of freedom, so that each such act actualizes the profound freedom of self-choice. Judge William declares that in his defense of either/or he is "fighting for freedom," and this echoes Victor Eremita's concern to preserve a region of secret inwardness by defending it from mediation's demands of rationalization and externalization. It is true, the Judge concedes, that a human being is a part of nature and a part of history, but he also possesses a freedom that is untouched by these forces: "while nature is created out of nothing, while I myself as an immediate personality am created out of nothing, as a free spirit I am born of the principle of contradiction, or born by the fact that I choose myself."[14] Freedom is not an "immediate" aspect of man *because it is a movement*. It is something—a form of consciousness—which comes into being, which is "born" from the individual's confrontation with either/or. Freedom *brings itself to birth*; it is a self-movement whereby the individual's consciousness undergoes a qualitative transformation: "when the passion of freedom is aroused, the self ... becomes himself, quite the same self as he was before ... and yet he becomes another, for the choice permeates everything and transforms it."[15]

The self-choice involved in becoming ethical effects its transformation by creating *significance*. In contrast to the aesthete's indifference, which renders him incapable of making a meaningful decision, the ethical individual can ground his choices upon the either/or of good and evil. Affirming this distinction between good and evil, and applying it to one's own actions, is a task for freedom. "How is it possible that the difference between good and evil emerges?" asks Judge William—in other words, how does one make the movement into the ethical?

> Is it an affair for thought? No. With this I have again reached . . . the question of why it could seem as if philosophy had abolished the principle of contradiction, when as a matter of fact it had not got so far as that. In the act of thinking, my relation to the thing thought is one of necessity, but precisely for this reason the difference between good and evil does not exist.[16]

Because good and evil are not the kind of things that already *are*, argues Judge William, they cannot be subjected to a logical dialectic. Logic deals with what is, with the necessary, whereas good and evil are effects of the will. This will is a principle of individuation: it is a being's capacity or power for self-movement. In becoming ethical, consciousness becomes *willful*. This subjective, willful consciousness can be contrasted with the philosophical consciousness which, claims the judge, denies the principle of contradiction "in order to abolish the factor of self-determination in thinking," and asserts its necessity and immanence by expressing *my* thinking in terms of "the self-thinking of the absolute in me." This insistence on necessity renders Hegelian philosophy incapable of confronting the ethical, because "such is not the case with the good. The good *is* for the fact that I will it, and apart from my willing it, it has no existence. This is the expression for freedom." This also applies to evil: it *is* only as the result of a person's will. Judge William makes it clear that he is not here suggesting that the difference between good and evil is merely subjective, but that, on the contrary, "the absolute validity of these distinctions is affirmed . . . and this is freedom."[17]

The distinction between necessity and freedom, which Kierkegaard invokes when he contrasts Hegelian or aesthetic movement with his own account of becoming ethical, is linked to another distinction—between the past and the future. While the aesthete exhibits a melancholy preoccupation with the past, Judge William emphasizes the priority of the future. Ethical questions, which are precipitated by one's acceptance of either/or, of "the reality of the act of choice," are concerned with the future: they ask not about what is or what has been, but about "what I am to do." There seems to be an essential connection between the existential principle of contradiction, freedom, and the future: "As truly as there is a future, just so truly is there an either/or . . . For freedom, therefore, I am fighting; I am fighting for the future, for either/or."[18]

The task of freedom is to make one's future one's own. Using the metaphor of a captain steering a ship, Judge William contrasts the aesthete's existential drifting with a purposeful movement forward.[19] This expresses a similar idea to his comment that, although the aesthetic individual does move through life, "no movement takes place within him," for he is carried along by external forces. Because of the fact of time—represented in the judge's analogy by the current of the sea and the force of the wind—the self is always in motion, but if one wants to *move oneself* one has to choose a direction and steer toward it. The moment of choice recurs constantly: there is no instant in which choice is suspended and there is time for deliberation, for while one is deciding which way to steer, the ship continues to move in the direction that has already been chosen. There is never a moment in which indifference is justified: "it is only an instant when it is indifferent whether he does this or that," and in fact this moment of deliberation, "like the Platonic instant, has no existence."[20] To continue in the direction one *has* chosen, without reaffirming its value by choosing it again and again, is to relinquish one's freedom. This means that freedom can never arise from something that is past.[21]

It is for this reason that Judge William criticizes both philosophy in general, and mediation in particular. In his view the aesthete personifies the weakness of Hegelian thought insofar as he cannot deal with ethical questions of freedom and the future. Even if philosophy is right to overcome the principle of contradiction, he argues, "this, however, surely cannot hold with respect to the future, for the oppositions must first be in existence before I can mediate them. But if the oppositions are there, then there must be an either/or."[22] This insistence that facing the future is essential to becoming ethical prepares the way for the further movement of becoming religious. Orienting oneself, subjectively, toward the future requires a kind of openness, for unlike the past the future is not bounded and determined, and cannot be rationalized. In other words, the future is unknown. This is not to say that it is empty: while the aesthete, when he looks to the future, sees only a vacuum, the ethical individual charges his future with significance through his passionate choices and commitments. The opposition between openness to the future (the unknown), and absorption in the past (as object of knowledge), is one variation of the opposition between transcendence and immanence that is at the heart of Kierkegaard's critique of Hegel. A movement toward the future, where logic holds no sway, is transcendent—it is a *leap*—and it is this movement that fuels Kierkegaard's attempt to banish Hegelian thinking from Christianity.

Either/Or ends with a short section headed "Ultimatum," in which Judge William offers the aesthete, for his edification, a sermon written by an elderly country pastor. Although this tends to be overlooked by readers (who may have given up halfway through the rather tedious second volume), it is the most profound and interesting part of the book. As the judge suggests, the sermon explores ideas that have already been discussed in his letters: "the expression, the form of presentation in which the thoughts are clothed, resembles the flowers which from one year to the next are the same and yet not the same; but the attitude, the movement, the position are unchanged."[23] Our commentary on *Either/Or* has of course focused on the issue of contradiction and on its significance for Kierkegaard in grounding the freedom of the existential movement with which he is concerned. However, the other major theme running right through the text is love: the aesthete and Judge William exhibit fundamentally different attitudes to life in general, but to love in particular. In the "Ultimatum" the themes of love and freedom are brought together as constitutive of the inwardness that produces a religious movement.

We have already considered Kierkegaard's description of *Either/Or* as "a polemic against the truth as knowledge," and have identified a thematic opposition between movement and stasis as one of the ways in which this polemic is expressed. Both the aesthetic consciousness and Hegelian philosophy are associated with existential impotence, as well as with reflection and necessity; the ethical individual, on the other hand, faces his freedom and takes responsibility for his actions. Ethical self-actualization requires recognition of the choice expressed by either/or, just as Aristotle's concept of kinesis must be grounded by the principle of contradiction. Becoming ethical—or in other words, realizing one's freedom—means being *empowered by difference*. The sermon repeats all these elements of the text: its opposition to knowledge, its affirmation of freedom, and its insistence on meaningful difference. However, it goes further than Judge William's account of the ethical insofar as it identifies the power of actualization that is expressed by freedom with *love*. "The truth as knowledge" is here opposed by a Christian interpretation of truth in terms of love.

The pastor's sermon addresses the issues of justice and sin-consciousness. With respect to this subject matter, it considers the alternatives of wanting to be in the right and wanting to be in the wrong: "When it is said, 'Thou shalt not contend with God,' the meaning of this is that you shall not wish to prove yourself in the right before Him. There is only one way of supporting the claim that you are in the right before God—by learning that you are in the wrong."[24] The desire to be right, to be in the right, may be understood as an essential characteristic of "the truth as knowledge"—to want to be in the wrong seems completely to undermine the project of knowing. Wishing to be in the wrong belongs to a different kind of truth: a truth that opposes necessity with freedom, and reason with faith.

The pastor suggests that an awareness of being always in the wrong before God is something to be desired. He acknowledges that being in the wrong is often very painful, but claims that it can also, at times, be edifying. These alternative responses to sin-consciousness are explained by the distinction between necessity and freedom: "by the fact that in the one case you are compelled to recognize that which in the other case you wish to recognize." This wishing to be in the wrong is, in turn, explained by love: "why was it you wished to be in the wrong with respect to a person? Because you loved. Why did you find this edifying? Because you loved." The pastor then compares the *willing* to be wrong that results from love with the *knowledge* that one is wrong that results "as a logical consequence" from the reflection that God is always in the right:

> You loved God, and hence your soul could find repose and joy only in the thought that you must always be in the wrong. It was not by toil of thought that you attained this recognition, neither was it forced upon you, for it is in love that you find your freedom . . . You did not attain the certainty that you were in the wrong as a deduction from the knowledge that God was always in the right, but from love's dearest and only wish.[25]

When one loves another (whether this other is human or divine), one is not made happy by finding fault with him. One wishes to admire, not to blame him—for one's own love suffers as a result of this blame. Wanting to be in the right is an assertion of the ego that makes love more difficult and painful; becoming religious involves surrendering this egotistical, defensive sense of self so that compassionate love flows out unhindered. As the pastor says, wishing to be always in the wrong "is the affair of love, hence of freedom": love is an expression of freedom because it originates from within, from inwardness—as opposed to logical reasoning, which remains outside one's subjectivity. The desire to be in the wrong "has its source in your whole being" and "springs from the love within you." Unleashing the power of freedom against the force of necessity is, as we have seen, crucial to *Either/Or*'s attack on Hegelian philosophy. In the "Ultimatum" we learn that this opposition between freedom and necessity is significant for Kierkegaard specifically with regard to love.

Reading *Either/Or* in the light of the theme of movement has shown how Kierkegaard's existential version of the principle of contradiction is the decisive factor in his account of freedom. This element of contradiction, or difference, is intensified in the sermon's discussion of the absolute difference between man and God. Just as Kierkegaard's either/or not only denotes a choice between the aesthetic and the ethical, but functions also to distinguish each of these forms of consciousness *internally*, so the religious consciousness invoked in the "Ultimatum" does not merely present a third alternative. Rather, it signifies an intensification of the irreducible difference inherent in either/or. The aesthete is *indifferent* to the possibilities available to him; the ethical individual recognizes *meaningful difference* such as that between good and evil; the religious person affirms an *absolute difference* between himself and God. The pastor argues that a finite approach to ethics, whereby one calculates one's righteousness "to a certain degree," and with regard to the judgments of men, leads only to self-doubt. In other words, doubt is the inevitable outcome of the project of knowledge. This doubt paralyses the individual, weakening his capacity to make decisions: "when he is in doubt, he has no power to act."[26]

The perspective of finitude recognizes relative differences—being to a certain degree in the right, to a certain degree in the wrong—and this always produces doubt. In the case of the relationship between man and God, difference is absolute: the pastor emphasizes that God is *essentially*, qualitatively greater than anything finite. In this case, there is no need for calculation and its attendant doubts, because God is *always* in the right:

> Only by an infinite relationship to God could the doubt be calmed, only by an infinitely free relationship to God could the anxiety be transformed into joy. He is in an infinite relationship to God when he recognizes that God is always in the right, in an infinitely free relationship to God when he recognizes that he himself is always in the wrong.[27]

Being in an infinite relationship to God means recognizing that He is absolutely different; being in an infinitely free relationship means that this recognition is filled with love, that God's difference is joyfully affirmed. While the doubts integral to finitude inhibit one's freedom by reducing one's powers of action, the belief that one is always in the wrong before God, because His love is greater than ours, is "an animating thought" that "makes a man glad to act." Here again we find a movement that depends on difference. Understanding God's absolute difference is edifying "in a double way," because it at once releases the individual from the paralysis of doubt, and "encourages and inspires to action."

The edification presented in *Either/Or* is aesthetic insofar as it is offered to one fictional character by another. However, the process of reading the text transforms the "you" addressed by the pastor's sermon into the reader herself—it is, of course, this reader to whom Kierkegaard offers the opportunity for edification. This means that the text itself aims to "animate to action," and indeed this kind of existential communication between author and reader is developed throughout Kierkegaard's authorship. "The reader who has absorbed the contents of the book will understand that the time has come for his move."[28] Kierkegaard aims not merely to describe his existential plane of motion, but to *institute* it, to bring it into being: for one who occupies this plane, communicating a truth means initiating an inward process of actualization within the individual reader.

In the final paragraph of the "Ultimatum"—which is also the conclusion of the entire book—the pastor makes it clear that edification is his criterion of truth: "only the truth that edifies is truth for you." Now, if edification means the empowering or strengthening (or "upbuilding") of the individual's inwardness, so that he is "animated to action," then this kind of movement must be essential to the subjective truth with which the pastor is concerned. Like Aristotle's kinesis, and like facing one's ethical freedom, edification seems also to involve a process of actualization. As we shall see in the chapters to follow, this idea is central to the account of truth which Kierkegaard opposes to knowledge. The pastor finishes his sermon by emphasizing that inward movement, rather than knowledge, constitutes the kind of truth that is really meaningful for the existing individual:

> One may have known a thing many times and acknowledged it, one may have willed a thing many times and attempted it; and yet it is only by the deep inward movements, only by the indescribable emotions of the heart, that for the first time you are convinced that what you have known belongs to you, that no power can take it from you; for only the truth which edifies is truth for you.

Chapter Five

Repetition: The Possibility of Motion

Kierkegaard wrote *Repetition* under the pseudonym "Constantin Constantius," and published it, together with Johannes de silentio's *Fear and Trembling*, on October 16, 1843. It makes sense to approach these two texts as companion pieces, for they are both concerned to reveal a disjunction between philosophy and existence, between social ethics and inwardness—and in each case "the truth as knowledge" is undermined by some kind of *movement*. Although *Repetition* begins where *Fear and Trembling* leaves off—by recalling the pre-Socratic debates about the possibility of motion—it presents a new interpretation of truth that helps to illuminate Johannes de silentio's analysis of Abraham, and for this reason we will explore it first.

The opening sentences of *Repetition* suggest an opposition between intellectual reflection, or "ideality," and movement. In response to the Eleatic philosophers' thesis that motion is unintelligible and therefore impossible, Diogenes enacts a movement:

> When the Eleatic School denied the possibility of motion, Diogenes, as everybody knows, stepped forth as an opponent. He *stepped* forth literally, for he said not a word, but merely walked several times back and forth, thinking that he had thereby refuted the philosophers.[1]

As Kierkegaard tells it, movement seems to triumph here, for Diogenes's "step forth" encourages us to look at the question of "the possibility of motion" in a new way. The opposition between ideality and movement is also, more broadly, an opposition between philosophy and existence—and there is certainly something existential about Diogenes's mode of demonstration. The struggle between philosophy and existence (often a struggle internal to the individual, especially to the intellectual, perhaps academic individual who is likely to be reading this text) is, we have seen, essential to Kierkegaard's dramatization of his conflict with Hegel. Here in *Repetition* this conflict revolves explicitly around the issue of movement.

Beginning the book in this way, with the dispute between Diogenes and the Eleatics, also accomplishes the repetition and renewal of the Greeks' questions about how movement and change are possible. These questions led to Aristotle's definition of kinesis as the transition from potentiality to actuality, which as we shall see is integral to Constantin Constantius's category of repetition. Like the Greeks, Constantin wants to know whether or not a certain sort of movement is possible: he proposes to take a trip to Berlin, where he has been once before, to see if he can achieve a repetition. In 1843 the Greeks' question of motion is not only repeated but renewed, for Kierkegaard asks about the movements of subjects, not objects—about internal, temporal beings. (The interiority and spirituality of the self is reflected by the transition, made explicit by Heidegger but long since in motion, from substance to time as philosophy's primary ontological category.) Diogenes is perhaps here to remind us that the question of motion finds its truth in some kind of stepping forth. With this in mind, Constantin travels to Berlin—but might we not expect a Kierkegaardian movement to involve a rather more *inward* journey?

The beginning of *Repetition* quoted above provides an interpretative key for the text as a whole. The renewal of the Greeks' question of motion, which implicitly invokes Aristotle's concept of kinesis, and the undermining of ideality by means of an existential movement, are essential to both the philosophical content and the narrative structure of this enigmatic little book. Constantin Constantius presents us with the "new category" of repetition that should, he claims, replace the concept of recollection that has dominated philosophy from Plato through to Hegel. This comparison between recollection and repetition echoes the opposition between idea and movement suggested by the anecdote about Diogenes: recollection is a mode of knowledge that retrieves the truth in the form of an idea, whereas repetition is a movement of becoming. As well as presenting us with these two opposing concepts, however, Constantin himself *participates in* the conflict between idea and movement that is dramatized through his troubled friendship with a younger man—and here Constantin, who represents an intellectual, philosophical point of view, is on the side of ideality. *Repetition*'s two protagonists are both concerned with questions of existential movement, but in different ways: Constantin treats repetition as an hypothesis and enquires in a pseudoscientific manner about its possibility; whereas the nameless young man comes to regard repetition as the transformation of his own existence, and he awaits it passionately.

Reading *Repetition* as a dramatized conflict between idea and movement clarifies the coherence of the text's narrative development, as well as the coherence of the philosophical concepts that are raised within this story. Like Judge William and the aesthete in *Either/Or*, Constantin and the young man are personifications of existential positions: Constantin is an intellectual, an abstract thinker, whereas the young man is a lover, a fiancé, whose self-awakening precipitates an ethical crisis. (Each resembles, of course, an aspect of Kierkegaard himself.) They differ significantly from *Either/Or*'s characters, however, insofar as they both undergo quite substantial self-development as the narrative unfolds. This in turn produces changes in the way they relate to one another, whereas in *Either/Or* there is no such interaction. In this way, the theme of movement is more comprehensively worked through in *Repetition*: as well as discussing the question of movement and reflecting divergent attitudes toward it, the characters are themselves in motion—and in each case, their existential development turns on the aporia of repetition. Kierkegaard's pseudonyms, personalities, and heroes are dynamic positions on the plane of inwardness whose movements accomplish certain transitions, relationships, and realizations. Constantin first appears proclaiming his new concept, set to take the philosophical world by storm; whereas by the end of the book he abandons repetition and "renounces all theorizing." The young fiancé is introduced as a melancholy, aesthetic character submerged in an idealistic romance, seeking Constantin's advice; after his crisis, he does not allow Constantin to contact him and, inspired by the Book of Job, longs for a repetition. The conflict between these two characters can be interpreted as the internal struggle of an individual whose attitude to philosophical reflection changes when he finds himself in an ethical situation. Through the course of *Repetition*, both the disinterested intellectual and the passionate existential aspects of this individual find their appropriate relationship to repetition: the former withdraws, while the latter is renewed and strengthened.

Considering this narrative framework allows us to analyze the concept of repetition within the context of the text's dramatic movements. These two aspects illuminate one another, and exploring them both will help us to appreciate the literary and philosophical originality of *Repetition*. We will begin by examining the category of repetition from Constantin's perspective—a detached, intellectual perspective that turns out to inhibit his attempt to discover the movement of repetition in "real life." Then we will turn to the young man's existential encounter with repetition, which distances him from Constantin's theoretical approach to life. Finally, we shall consider the dynamic, actualizing qualities of the text itself, exploring the ways in which it attempts to *bring its ideas into existence.*

∞

What does Kierkegaard mean by repetition? That repetition is more than a concept is integral to its meaning, for, as a movement, repetition exceeds ideality. This seems to complicate the way we can discuss repetition—after all, in order to do so Kierkegaard wrote a strange, elusive book that is more like an experimental novel than a conventional philosophical treatise. Nevertheless, although Constantin's presentation of repetition as a philosophical category may not adequately express its full significance, we can and must attempt to elucidate repetition philosophically. I would prefer to describe repetition as a way of being (becoming) and as a form of consciousness, suggestive of a particular plane of motion, rather than as a concept that can be extracted from its literary context and analyzed systematically. But before we explore how repetition is expressed through the text as a whole, and in particular through the developments and interactions of the characters of Constantin and the young man, it will be helpful to clarify its philosophical significance as much as possible.

So, what is repetition? The first thing that Constantin says about it is that "repetition is a decisive expression for what 'recollection' was for the Greeks,"[2] and he goes on to define repetition in opposition to recollection. This suggests that these two concepts have something in common, while also differing significantly from one another. In some sense, recollection and repetition are the same kind of thing—"the same movement, only in opposite directions."

For the Greeks—which here means, more precisely, for Socrates and Plato—recollection was a theory of knowledge. In other words, it signifies a way of finding the truth, a process through which truth is realized. Both recollection and repetition are ways of reaching truth, and they differ insofar as each belongs to a different consciousness of what this truth is and where it can be found. As philosophical categories of truth, recollection and repetition are both defined in terms of temporal movements. This, indeed, is expressed in the everyday sense of the words: someone who recollects is thinking about the past, retrieving an image of a passed actuality, whereas repetition signifies something that has passed away becoming actual once again. Recollection and repetition relate to the past in different ways: that which is recollected is already finished, complete within itself, so that it is in some sense static. On the other hand, when something is repeated it is reenacted, brought into existence; it is not only represented as an idea, but recreated as a reality. As philosophical terms, the Greek recollection and the "modern" repetition denote processes toward the truth that express entirely different forms of self-consciousness, different interpretations of time, different ontologies—in short, different truths.

The Platonic doctrine of recollection is based on an understanding of truth as atemporal and eternal. The object of recollection is the realm of Ideas, or Forms, and the individual relates to this realm by means of his immortal, rational soul. This means that truth is in no way affected by the passing of time, or by the individual's finite, situated existence. The process of recollection begins within subjectivity, but its goal is the same for every subject: the individual who recollects is connected to the universal, to a truth that is valid for all (for all beings, and for all time). This movement of knowledge takes the individual from the captivating illusions of the physical world to the eternal reality of the Ideas. In recollection, the truth is grasped through an *idealizing movement*: as Kierkegaard had already remarked in his dissertation *The Concept of Irony*, "Socrates ferried the individual from reality over to ideality."[3] The Platonic philosopher turns toward an eternal realm where the soul has existed prior to its particular incarnation. Recollection—like all knowledge, in fact—is immanent, insofar as it deals with what *is*, rather than with what comes into being.[4]

Constantin tells us that, in contrast to recollection, "repetition is always a transcendence."[5] While recollection leads to the truth as *knowledge*, repetition is concerned with a truth that belongs to *life*: "When the Greeks said that all knowledge is recollection they affirmed that all that is has been; when one says that life is a repetition one affirms that existence which has been now becomes."[6] Constantin adds that "recollection is the pagan life-view; repetition is the modern life-view," which implies that he understands "modern" to involve a specifically Christian consciousness. While the Greek philosopher found the truth in an eternity that existed before his birth, the Christian looks forward to an eternity to come after his death. This eternal life is, of course, the truth that Jesus proclaims. So, both recollection and repetition are movements of truth: recollection moves toward a past eternity, and repetition moves toward a future eternity. This illuminates Constantin's remark that "recollection and repetition are the same movement, only in opposite directions."[7]

Kierkegaard's point here is not simply to criticize the Greek notion of recollection, for from his historical perspective he views this as a natural expression of the pagan mentality. However, he finds the recollective mode of knowledge inadequate as a way of reaching the truth of Christianity—and in particular he wants to challenge the Hegelian claim to comprehend the whole of Absolute Spirit, including Christian faith and doctrine, within a philosophical system.[8] Later, in the *Postscript*, Kierkegaard's pseudonym describes speculative philosophy as "a pagan reminiscence against which there is nothing to object to if it straightforwardly breaks with Christianity, but much to object to if it assumes to be Christianity."[9] For Kierkegaard, recollection is incompatible with Christianity because it signifies immanence, and a grasp of the truth only in terms of knowledge. The idealizing movement of knowing cannot realize the kind of truth essential to Christianity—a truth incarnated in Jesus; a truth that literally *comes into being*; a truth defined, throughout the pseudonymous works, in terms of the subjectivity of the existing individual. *Repetition*, like *Either/Or*, is "a polemic against the truth as knowledge" that aims to "transform everything into inwardness."

∞

Constantin contrasts both repetition and recollection with a third philosophical category: Hegelian mediation. This is also a movement of knowing, a way of reaching the truth. Because Hegel's philosophy is based on an understanding of truth as in process, rather than as a fixed, transcendent reality outside the world of becoming, mediation is supposed to be a "modern" version of recollection. However, Kierkegaard insists that mediation is not a real movement. Recollection moves from finite, situated existence to ideality, and repetition moves from ideality to existence—but the principle of mediation, according to Kierkegaard, functions *within* ideality, within reflection, and is therefore not a movement in the sense of a qualitative transition. For this reason, Constantin states that "properly it is repetition which by mistake has been called mediation." Having rejected this Hegelian concept of movement, Constantin advises its advocates to consider "the Greek reflection upon the concept of *kinesis*."[10]

This reference to kinesis reaches the crux of repetition's significance. If we return, for a moment, to the question of motion that lies at the root of Aristotle's concept of kinesis—as, indeed, the opening sentence of *Repetition* suggests we do—we find a connection between movement and truth. All philosophers pose their questions about truth in a changing world (and they are themselves changing continually as they do so): movement is the truth of existence, and yet it turns truth—at least, the truth as knowledge—into a problem, something fugitive and troubling. The Greeks' questions about "the possibility of motion" ask about how we are to grasp and articulate this truth of becoming—and this is the problem that is raised again by Constantin's enquiry into repetition.

Philosophers tend to agree that, as Socrates teaches, the truth must be grasped in the form of an idea, through an idealizing movement. For Kierkegaard, however, the essential expression for movement, for the truth of existence *as* movement, as becoming, is Aristotle's concept of kinesis: the transition from potentiality to actuality. This category of movement is integral to Aristotle's interpretation of existence in terms of substance. As Aristotle's most basic ontological concept, substance signifies that which exists, that which is individual and free—and these attributes are precisely its kinesis, its specific power of becoming. No wonder then that Kierkegaard, who argues against Hegel that truth is the task of a human subject who is constituted above all by his existence, his individuality, and his freedom, repeats Aristotle's emphasis on kinesis. Although Hegel's logic attempts to provide a dynamic form of thought, nothing actually *comes into being* through this purely intellectual process. The dialectic moves from one concept to another (just as the aesthete moves from one possibility to another without actualizing any of them), and these are transitions of necessity rather than freedom, of immanence rather than transcendence. Kierkegaard's crucial point is this: if a real movement, a movement expressing the truth of becoming, has to be a kinesis, then *the truth involves the transition from potentiality to actuality*. For Kierkegaard, truth implies actualization: an idea or possibility being brought into existence, as in repetition, rather than the transition from existence to idea that occurs in recollection ("the same movement, only in opposite directions").

The connection between kinesis and repetition is only hinted at in the text itself, and attentive, sympathetic reading is required to find between recollection and repetition the distinction, the difference, that is precisely this movement of actualization. A few months after the publication of *Repetition*, Heiberg wrote a lukewarm review of the book that, not surprisingly, betrays much confusion. Heiberg assumed that the category of repetition applies to the cyclical processes of the natural world, rather than to the interior, spiritual processes of human existence—and this misunderstanding prompted Kierkegaard, through his pseudonym, to explain himself more fully. Addressing Heiberg, Constantin makes the affinity between repetition and Aristotle's concept of kinesis much more explicit:

> If motion is allowed in relation to repetition in the sphere of freedom, then its development in this sphere is different from logical development in this respect, that *transition is a becoming*. In the sphere of logic, transition is mute, in the sphere of freedom it *becomes*. . . . In the sphere of freedom, there is possibility, and actuality emerges as a transcendency. Therefore when even Aristotle said that the transition from possibility to actuality is a *kinesis* he was not talking about logical possibility and actuality but about the possibility and actuality of freedom, and therefore he quite rightly posits motion.[11]

In his response to Heiberg, Constantin clarifies that his category of repetition applies to "the sphere of individual freedom," and emphasizes that "repetition is not merely for contemplation, but . . . is the task of freedom . . . It signifies freedom itself." This suggests a connection between repetition, as a movement toward the truth, and the process of becoming ethical that is described by Judge William: repetition is a movement of freedom that is directed toward the future. Constantin also suggests—again echoing Judge William—that this movement occurs within inwardness: repetition is "the most inward problem," and must be found "within the individual," where "the question is not about the repetition of something outward, but about the repetition of his freedom."

As we have seen, Kierkegaard interprets human freedom in terms of an actualizing movement. Being free means being capable of becoming, having the power to actualize oneself in the way one chooses. This notion of power is connected to Kierkegaard's idea of transcendence, which he understands as the coming into being of the new. Just as kinesis signifies the actualization of a new quality, so repetition "has the character of novelty."[12] In this way, the immanence (and impotence) of Hegelian mediation is opposed by the free, transcendent movement of repetition.

Constantin's response to Heiberg's review is particularly helpful in clarifying this opposition between immanence and transcendence that seems to lie at the heart of the question of movement raised by *Repetition*. Heiberg had suggested that the application of the category of repetition to the natural world "is evident from the fact that [the author] associates repetition with a concept of natural philosophy, viz. *motion*." This remark prompts Constantin to launch into an attack on Hegelian mediation:

> Motion also belongs in the sphere of spirit. In our days they have even gone so far as to want to introduce motion into logic. There they have called repetition 'mediation.' Motion, however, is a concept which logic

cannot endure. Hence mediation must be understood in relation to immanence. Thus understood, mediation cannot be employed at all in the sphere of freedom, where the next thing constantly emerges, not by virtue of immanence but of transcendence.

Constantin claims that Hegelian philosophy transfers the concept of mediation from logic to the sphere of freedom, and that this is problematic because it "makes the transcendency of motion illusory." He suggests that using the term "repetition" to describe spiritual motion will avoid this confusion and will help to preserve a clear concept of transcendence. This implies that repetition signifies a transcendent movement, or a transition to transcendence: "a religious movement by virtue of the absurd, which comes to pass when it has reached the borders of the marvelous."

Repetition signifies the coming into being of the new—but it also expresses the continuity of existence through time. Even in ancient Greek philosophy, the question of motion is also the question of self-identity. For Heraclitus, for example, the claim that everything is motion implies the dissolution of individuality, at least on a metaphysical level. Returning to *Repetition*, we find Constantin suggesting that God's creation of the world involves the actualizing movement of repetition:

> If God himself had not willed repetition, the world would never have come into existence. He would either have followed the light plans of hope, or he would have recalled it all and conserved it in recollection. This he did not do, therefore the world endures, and it endures for the fact that it is a repetition.[13]

This example of repetition suggests the influence of Leibniz, whose *Theodicy* Kierkegaard studied during 1842 and 1843. On the first page of *Repetition*, Constantin asserts that "modern philosophy will teach that the whole of life is a repetition. The only philosopher who has had an intimation of this was Leibniz"—and in his journal Kierkegaard notes his sympathy with the understanding of transition expressed in Leibniz's doctrine of the "pre-established harmony" of the world.[14] The *Theodicy* probably appealed to Kierkegaard because its account of God's creative power leaves room for the individual's freedom: when a person actualizes a possibility in his life, his self-expression coincides with God's determination, so that "the divine activity is repeated in the activity of the monad."[15]

Constantin's suggestion that the world endures because it is a repetition implies that self-identity is grounded on movement, on becoming (which in turn is grounded on difference, on newness). Endurance signifies persistence through time, but this must be distinguished from the drifting, linear motion that Kierkegaard associates with aesthetic existence (expressed, for example, by Judge William's metaphor of a ship without a captain). Concrete existence, unlike the necessary being with which logic deals, has reality only insofar as it continues to be actualized at every moment. Existence is always *coming into existence*, arising and passing away and arising again at unfathomable speed. So for an existing thing to endure—to *be itself*—it must be repeatedly renewed, for without this actualizing movement it falls into non-being.

The concept of renewal captures the sense that identity and change, sameness and difference, are held together in the continual motion of existence. Repetition expresses that rather paradoxical element which becomes integral to Kierkegaard's later accounts of truth: remaining *the same* always implies *difference*—the basic temporal differentiation between 'then' and 'now'—because even if two beings (one past and the other present) are externally, apparently the same, internally they are already differentiated through the movement of repetition itself.[16]

This brings us back to the point, which Constantin takes care to emphasize in his response to Heiberg, that repetition is an inward movement. This means that it is a movement of intensification, of deepening, within the 'heart' or the 'soul' of the individual: Constantin describes repetition as "consciousness raised to the second power." Repetition is a dynamic intensity, an expression of power: a repetition is not external to the original, simply added on to it, but is rather the product of this origin, its self-expression. (As Deleuze explains in *Difference and Repetition*, repetitions "do not add a second or third time to the first, but carry the first time to the 'nth' power . . . it is not Federation Day which commemorates or represents the fall of the Bastille, but the fall of the Bastille which celebrates and repeats in advance all the Federation Days; or Monet's water lily which repeats all the others."[17] A more relevant illustration in the present context is the way in which religious teachings repeat themselves: the words of, say, Jesus or the Buddha are so powerful that they reverberate through centuries and across continents.) As an inward, intensifying movement, repetition expresses the spiritual power of a singular thing. To put it another way, the measure of a being's significance is its power to repeat itself, to renew itself, to project itself forward, to actualize itself again. This movement, as Constantin suggests, is important in the light of the Christian doctrine of atonement: Jesus' perfect penitence, and the complete forgiveness this receives, repeat themselves within his less than perfect followers.[18]

One way of making sense of this difficult concept of repetition is through the example of a romantic relationship between two people—say, a marriage (and this, of course, is always a pertinent analogy in the case of Kierkegaard's thought). Marriage does not happen once and for all, on the wedding day, but has to be continually repeated, reactualized, if it is to remain meaningful, true, or authentic. This becomes explicit when tensions latent within the union build up to a moment of crisis, bringing the whole relationship into question: resolution will come through either dissolution or renewal. In the case of renewal, the union is reaffirmed, chosen again, and through this it is consolidated and deepened; the relationship expresses its power, its significance, by repeating itself.

Repetition is a philosophical category, and an interpretation of truth, that Kierkegaard creates in order to articulate, more fully than recollection or mediation, "the task of becoming a Christian." Repetition expresses the Christian understanding of faith as a kind of spiritual rebirth—becoming a Christian is often described in terms of being "born again," beginning one's life in a new way. This movement of renewal challenges the understanding of time as immanent, as an unbroken continuity, which underlies the theories of recollection and mediation. A repetition is preceded by some kind of break; it signals a new beginning; it articulates difference, in the form of "more than once." (Kierkegaard later replaces repetition with the category of "the moment": central to Christianity, grounding the possibility of all things becoming new, "is the fullness of time, is the instant as eternity, and yet this eternity is at once the future and the past."[19] In *Philosophical Fragments*, Climacus's insistence on the significance of "the moment" points beyond Socratic immanence, just as Constantin's concept of repetition is supposed to break with the immanence associated with recollection. When a moment in time is genuinely decisive—when it actually forms the future—temporal existence becomes more than a mere occasion for knowledge, more than a point of departure to ideality.) For Kierkegaard, the Christian eternal differs from the Platonic eternal insofar as it is in motion: unlike a realm of fixed Ideas, God is a *power* that can break into history and create something new.

The movement of repetition expresses both sides of Christian faith—the movements of God (creation, incarnation, grace) and the movements of the individual (rebirth, passionate commitment, receiving God's love). These 'two sides' of faith might be called its objective and subjective aspects—although this opposition is loaded with philosophical and theological controversy—but their being brought together through the category of repetition gives some indication of the way in which they are inseparable, for becoming a Christian means bringing into being a reciprocal relationship between man and God. It is not so much that "a Christian" is something one becomes, as that becoming is itself the medium, the element of Christianity. To live constantly in relation to God is to know that one's existence is not one's own but belongs to God, that one possesses nothing and can claim nothing—for understanding and affirming this is the condition for receiving a self, a life, and a world as a gift from God. This gift is received but never held: it is lost as soon as it is gained, so that it can be given again. In this way the individual's relationship to God can be repeatedly actualized, repeatedly renewed, and can thus endure through time. Gift and loss, receiving and giving away, constitute the basic differential element of Christian repetition.

∞

My attempt to explain Constantin's concept of repetition has identified its various aspects and indicated some of the ways in which these cohere. We may say that repetition is a movement that is associated with truth, with freedom, with temporal becoming, and with transcendence; like Aristotle's kinesis, it signifies a process of actualization. Repetition is an inward movement, an intensification, an expression of spiritual power. Applied to the existing individual, it denotes a kind of kinesis of the self, a continual movement of coming into being. We have not yet, however, discovered *how* this movement happens—and so Constantin's question about the possibility of motion remains open. Because it occurs *in inwardness*, repetition eludes objective description; it signifies a way of existing that is quite distinct from philosophical reflection. This existential significance of repetition is illuminated by the ways in which it is encountered from the different perspectives of the book's two principal characters.

One of the key themes of *Repetition* is the role of philosophy in relation to the individual's existential development—or, in other words, in relation to the movement of repetition. Because Constantin personifies philosophy, and the fiancé personifies subjective, engaged existence, the interactions of these two men reflect Kierkegaard's view of the relationship between philosophical thought and existential motion.

Constantin Constantius presents repetition as a new philosophical category. In the first part of the book, he claims that this category is vital to modern thought, because it is more expressive of the movement of life than the Greek concept of recollection. However, there is a stark contrast between Constantin's enthusiastic discussion of repetition and his failure actually to achieve a repetition of his past experience during his second trip to Berlin. He stays at the same hotel as before, sees the same play at the theater, drinks coffee in the same café, and eats in the same restaurant—but he fails to recapture any of his fondly remembered experiences. Having met only with frustration at every turn, Constantin eventually gives up and admits defeat: "it is lucky that the young man does not seek any enlightenment from me, for I have abandoned my theory, I am adrift."[20] This acceptance of failure is, ironically, the greatest existential movement that Constantin accomplishes, for he has finally realized that repetition is a "transcendent," "religious" movement.

Constantin's journey to Berlin is in fact an empty parody of repetition. His failure indicates that he has searched for repetition in the wrong place, and in the wrong way. He tries to reproduce a past that is already idealized, whereas his remembered happiness could only be repeated through experiencing something new. With the disinterested, experimental attitude of a scientist, Constantin approaches repetition as an hypothesis that can be subjected to empirical validation; with the detachment of an actor, he *goes through the motions* of seeking a repetition in Berlin. Acting in this way, he disregards his own inwardness: he treats himself as a general case, as subject to a law that exemplifies the possibility of repetition for anyone, rather than as a unique, particular individual. Repetition is opposed to the process of generalization through which concepts—whether scientific or philosophical—operate; as we have seen, repetition is a spiritual category that expresses the intensification of a singular power, as opposed to the accumulation of several externally related instances of 'the same thing.'

Constantin shares some of the characteristics that have already been exhibited by the aesthete in *Either/Or*—where, we may recall, Kierkegaard attempts to position philosophical reflection within the aesthetic sphere of existence. The name "Constantin Constantius" emphasizes the stasis of intellectual life; he has, he tells us, "a great distrust of upheavals." More importantly, he is preoccupied with external things: his failure to find repetition by going to Berlin is due to his inability to understand that it is an inward movement. This point is clarified in Constantin's response to Heiberg: "the confusion consists in the fact that the most inward problem is here expressed in an outward way, as though repetition, if it were possible, might be found outside the individual." When he returns home, Constantin again seeks repetition in something external—the ordered arrangement of his house—but he is distressed to find that his home has been turned upside down. At this point the scene becomes comical and rather absurd, and Kierkegaard seems to be poking fun at an intellectual's inability to cope with movement and change. Once order has been restored, Constantin describes with satisfaction the resumption of his domestic routine: "everything which was not able to move stood in its precise place, and what was able to go went its accustomed way—my parlour clock, my servant and myself, who with measured tread walked back and forth across the floor."[21]

Constantin's preference for things that can be ordered, quantified, and measured is further illustrated by his tendency to avoid women, who are difficult to categorize:

> Generally a woman lacks the logical consistency which is necessary if one is to hold another human being in admiration or contempt. She deceives herself before she deceives another, and therefore one has no scale to judge her by . . . the idea as measuring rod is the surest scale in the world.[22]

In other words, Constantin finds it difficult to interact with anything, or anyone, which lacks the transparency of a concept. This illustrates Kierkegaard's view that philosophy, armed with its rational "measuring rod," achieves only a quantitative understanding of existence, and is unable to cope with the subtle complexities of human life (self-deceptions and so on) that are represented here by the feminine character. Quantitative measurements cannot do justice to the deep, inward movements of existence.

Constantin tells us that he "is inclined to remain a detached observer in relation to people," and that he has taught himself "to have only an ideal interest in people." This disinterested attitude to existence, and preference for ideality, is in contrast to his presentation of repetition as characterized by "interest," "reality," and "the seriousness of life." Constantin represents philosophy itself insofar as he can form only an idea of reality. This purely intellectual relationship to life has no existential power: Constantin can describe the movement of repetition, but he cannot make one. It is philosophy itself (or at least, Kierkegaard's caricature of it) that speaks when Constantin says, "a religious movement I am unable to make, it is contrary to my nature."[23]

Through his involvement with the fiancé, however, Constantin loses confidence in intellectual reflection and is unable to maintain his attitude of indifference to others. Toward the end of *Repetition*, he tells us that "the young man, because of my interest in him, put me a bit out of my pendulum-regularity."[24] The fiancé's situation, in which the question of repetition reaches its real, existential significance, forces Constantin out of his habit of relating to others only ideally—and in this way he ceases to be merely an intellectual, a philosopher, and becomes a little more 'authentically' human. Earlier, Constantin had claimed that "repetition is the *interest* of metaphysics, and at the same time the interest upon which metaphysics founders," and now, insofar as he himself personifies metaphysics, he "founders" by becoming interested in the young man. He gives up his enquiry into repetition and "withdraws from theorizing." In his final address to the reader Constantin emphasizes his intention to step aside and allow the fiancé to take center stage: "I am only a serviceable spirit . . . Every movement I have made was merely for the sake of throwing light upon him." From Kierkegaard's point of view, this expresses an anti-Hegelian movement: philosophy renounces its sovereignty for the sake of an existing individual. Although Constantin's character is complex—and often, it seems, contradictory—one of his functions is to perform a movement of resignation. As Johannes de silentio argues in *Fear and Trembling*, this self-renunciation is "the highest movement" that immanence, or rationality, is capable of making.

∞

Constantin's concept of repetition signifies that truth involves a movement of becoming, of actualization. The character of the fiancé *exemplifies in existence* what Constantin describes in more abstract terms: finding himself in an ethical situation where it seems impossible to do the right thing, he discovers the significance of repetition. This discovery involves an encounter with difference, inwardness, faith and love, which as we shall see are constitutive of the truth as repetition—the truth belonging to existential subjectivity that Kierkegaard wishes to oppose to "the truth as knowledge." Coming together in the fiancé's situation, the elements of difference, inwardness, faith, and love provide a coherent articulation of Kierkegaard's subjective plane of motion, while resisting the idealizing direction of philosophical thought. This resistance is, in fact, integral to their significance—and so the young man's encounter with this new, existential form of truth is accompanied by a movement away from Constantin, who personifies ideality. This means that the fiancé's relationship to Constantin is rather ambivalent: although the pseudonym has "brought him into being" to exemplify the movement of repetition, in order actually to make this movement he has to reject Constantin's intellectual perspective.

Moving on from aesthetic ideality, becoming ethical, requires—as we saw in the previous chapter—recognition of the *difference* that is inherent in the continually renewed moment of decision: either/or. For Kierkegaard, difference becomes an existential category rather than just an abstract concept: he opposes difference to *indifference* as well as to sameness. Constantin is incapable of repetition because he seeks to establish the constancy of sameness in his everyday life; because, by confining himself to ideality, he tries to avoid the difference that is inherent in becoming. In the case of the young man, the opening-up of inwardness that constitutes his path to the truth begins with the discovery of this difference. As his situation develops, he experiences difference as "becoming another man," as self-contradiction, as an inability to communicate with others, as exemption from the judgments of ethics, and finally as repetition.

At its simplest, the young man's situation is this: *he has changed his mind.* He realizes that he cannot commit himself wholeheartedly to his fiancée, for he has become aware that he lacks freedom, and that he desires it. His engagement has become a "monstrous untruth," because he himself has changed, and in a way he could not have foreseen. This situation forces him to recognize that he *exists*—that he is in a process of becoming, that he is free—and this recognition signifies the transition from an aesthetic to an ethical form of consciousness. Turning inward, the young man finds the movement of renewal, of becoming different, which constitutes his self. His subjectivity—his truth—is in motion because it is free, because it continually requires a choice to be made (and this echoes, on an existentialist plane, Aristotle's insight that motion requires the principle of contradiction).

The fiancé is no longer the man who wanted to marry his "beloved"; he desires his freedom, and to marry now would be deceitful—but he has also deceived the girl by breaking his promise to her. Because he is in motion, the truth is also in motion. What use, now, is the Platonic doctrine that truth is an eternal, unchanging idea, separate from the existing individual? Instead, the young man requires repetition, a kind of truth that, as Constantin has explained, "affirms that the existence which has been *now becomes.*" Only a movement can redeem the young man, and so he attempts to change himself, to "trim himself" into a suitable husband. When his repetition finally occurs it does indeed change the situation again, and once more in an unexpected way: the girl gets engaged to someone else, releasing the young man from the ethical dilemma that seemed to prevent him from acting truthfully. As Constantin suggests, "repetition is the solution contained in every ethical view."[25]

The young man seeks to exempt himself from the judgments of ethics, as well as from Constantin's intellectual point of view. Because he has acted according to his awareness of the truth—*as this truth has changed*—the fiancé maintains, in opposition to ethics, that his actions are justified. It is the fact of difference, of his "becoming another man," that grounds the young man's claim upon the ethical. In the end, although Constantin's detached, intellectual perspective is distinct from the ethical perspective (and, for Kierkegaard, in some sense inferior to it), the two are integrally related. The conceptual and scientific laws which Constantin presupposes in his experiment in repetition, and which govern his habitual existence—that is, the laws under which he seeks reproduction of the same—are variations of the moral law that judges the fiancé's actions. All these laws belong to an order of generality, of universality, of sameness—in short, to what Kierkegaard regards as knowledge—as opposed to repetition's dynamic of difference, newness, and singularity. As Emmanuel Levinas suggests, the ethical for Kierkegaard is essentially general: "the individuality of the self would be dissipated, according to him, in any rule that was valid for everyone. Generality could neither contain nor express the secrets of the self."[26] Deleuze also emphasizes that "repetition is always a transgression" that denounces the nominal or general character of the law "in favor of a more profound and more artistic reality."[27] In the case of Kierkegaardian repetition, the "reality" that it produces is *inwardness*—a reality that is "profound" and "artistic" because its movement at once *deepens* the self and *creates* it anew.

Constantin has already emphasized that repetition is an inward movement, and the young man confirms that "the movement goes on in one's interior."[28] As an actualizing movement (a movement "in the opposite direction" to the truth as knowledge), repetition is a *creative* turning-inwards: it signifies the dynamic opening-up *of* inwardness, *of* subjectivity. In other words, this movement, in bringing inwardness into being, *is* inwardness itself. It is this process of becoming-inward that takes place in the fiancé's situation, reflecting his development from an aesthetic attitude, through an encounter with ethics, to his claim to be an exception to ethical judgments.

When Constantin introduces us to the young man, the first thing we are told about him is that he is melancholy. This suggests a comparison with the aesthete of *Either/Or*: as we saw in the previous chapter, melancholy is a symptom of the aesthetic state of indifference and impotence with regard to existence. *Repetition*'s young man is rather less cynical and nihilistic than *Either/Or*'s aesthete—as, indeed, is evident from the fact that he has fallen in love and become engaged. However, throughout this period of romance the fiancé's melancholy continues; he remains an aesthetic character insofar as his life is dominated by ideality. Constantin observes that the young man *recollects* his love: he relates to his "beloved" as an idea, rather than as another existing, subjective person. Like other Kierkegaardian fiancées, 'she' is always absent from the text, little known except as the cause of her lover's melancholy; she seems to have significance to the young man only in terms of his own moods. As Constantin recognizes, "in reality her existence or non-existence was in a certain sense of no importance to him, only it was his melancholy which found delight in rendering life enchanting to her."[29] Later, when he looks back on his engagement, the young man realizes that "the reality in which she is to find significance is for me only a shadow which runs alongside of my proper spiritual reality."[30] To describe the fiancé as "aesthetic" or "recollective" is to suggest that he is not free ("his melancholy ensnared him more and more"), freedom here meaning a power for actualization, for self-movement. Aesthetic movement, by contrast, occurs within or toward ideality.

During his aesthetic phase the young man has an increasingly close relationship to Constantin—the personification of philosophical reflection. He visits Constantin at his house in order to distract himself from anxious thoughts about his "beloved," and the detached observer becomes his "confidant." Constantin's remark that he is the confidant of "so many like him" implies, as I have suggested, that he represents the disinterested, intellectual perspective *within the individual*, and that the opposition which develops between the two characters reflects the movement of the fiancé's consciousness beyond its idealizing, aesthetic tendency. The *difficulty* of this movement—of this emancipation from Constantin's influence—also suggests that the young man is contending with something that is part of himself. He feels drawn to Constantin, and finds the older man's calm intellectuality compelling even as it ceases to make sense to him.

As the fiancé's awareness of his situation develops, he awakens to his lack of freedom and then, immediately, to his desire to be free. This self-realization becomes complete when he expresses it to Constantin—and at precisely this moment, their relationship changes: "in the wildest outburst he cursed existence, his love and the darling girl. From that moment he came to my house no more . . . When he encountered me he avoided me, and if we met he never talked."[31] The young man's reticence signals the beginning of his turning-inward. As he emphasizes in his letters from Stockholm, the inability to communicate itself (resistance to language's *idealizing movement* of representation) is an essential feature of inwardness. In his final departure from Denmark the young man leaves Constantin behind, and will not allow a reply to the letters he writes to his "silent confidant." In this way he silences the voice of reason, whose grasp of truth in terms of the idea no longer has any meaning for him. From the new perspective of his struggle with ethics, the young man finds that Constantin's "cold common sense" expresses "mental derangement." His movement away from Constantin symbolizes the transformation taking place within his consciousness: the transition from ideality to actuality, from philosophy to existence, which is expressed by the concept of repetition—and which, indeed, we found in the opening sentences of the book.

Because it is resistant to ideality, knowledge, representation, and so on, the inward movement of repetition is not, for the most part, described explicitly, but is instead indicated metaphorically. For example, the interiority of the young man's movement is expressed indirectly by his physical immobility:

> Here I sit . . . I know only this, that I am sitting and that I have not budged from the spot . . . I know only this, that here I stay and that for a whole month I have remained *suspenso gradu* without drawing my foot towards me or making the least movement.[32]

The most coherent expression of the inwardness of repetition is provided by the imagery of the thunderstorm. In the young man's letters, this functions as a metaphor—borrowed from the story of Job—for his own consciousness. The gathering clouds symbolize suffering, the increasingly heavy demands that existence makes upon him: in the intensity of his situation he finds, like Job, "the passion of pain." The metaphor of the storm conveys the sense of increasing tension and accumulating power within the young man, through which his inwardness is deepened. When the storm breaks, everything changes: the kinetic energy is released, and the sky is cleared. This sky is like the individual's consciousness, which gathers the power to free itself. In the intensive movement of the storm, the 'space' of inwardness is opened up. Of course, this is metaphorical, since inward, intensive movement implies only temporality, not spatiality.

As the metaphor of the storm suggests, repetition is a movement of intensification: "consciousness raised to the second power."[33] Intensity within the individual can be equated with passion, with an awareness of the significance of one's existence that keeps one focused on actuality. It is Kierkegaard's preoccupation with spiritual power—the power that is required for "becoming a Christian"—that lies behind the themes of movement and passion in the pseudonymous texts. Power, or actualization, signifies existence and freedom—and, ultimately, the transcendent source of these—as opposed to the impotence of the aesthetic way of life.

Difference and change, inwardness and intensification, constitute the form of the truth as repetition. Less abstractly, *faith* and *love* are the content of this truth. Kierkegaard is concerned with the truth of fidelity, in the sense of *being true to* someone. His challenge to and transformation of philosophical thinking can be summed up in the simple contention that truth is not primarily that which one knows, but that which one *is*—or rather, that which one becomes. From the perspective of knowledge, truth is opposed to error; from the existential perspective of *Repetition*'s fiancé, truth is opposed to deceit. The crucial question for the fiancé is, *how is it possible to be true when he is changing, when he "becomes another man"?* And the answer that he finds, in the form of repetition, is that *the constancy of fidelity is grounded not on sameness, but on difference.* Because existence is temporal and therefore constantly changing, something can 'stay the same' only if it continually becomes new. This, indeed, is an expression of the individual's freedom. Whether the fidelity in question is truthfulness to another person, to God, or to oneself, this is the kind of truth that needs to be actualized repeatedly, rather than a necessary, static truth that merely 'is.'

This requirement of actualization, based on the priority of difference over sameness, is essential to love. As the sermon at the end of *Either/Or* suggests, "it is in love that you find yourself in freedom"; one can love only if one is free. Love is itself an actualizing power, because through love the individual makes the subjectivity of another a reality for himself. Love is also a movement of becoming-identical on the basis of difference—for Kierkegaard, this constitutes the profound and paradoxical truth of God's incarnation as an existing individual. At the heart of the opposition between recollection and repetition is a choice between a truth that operates according to the principle of identity or sameness (the generality of *law*), and a truth grounded by difference (the singularity of *love*). This clarifies the relevance of repetition for Christianity in particular, and illuminates Constantin's remark that "repetition is always a transcendence." Ultimately, the "more profound and more artistic reality" that Deleuze associates with the movement of repetition is, for Kierkegaard, a religious reality that has its source, its actualizing power, in love. This is why its degree of intensity is registered as passion, and not according to philosophy's "measuring rod."

The final twist in this tale is that *Repetition*'s fiancé falls short of this religious movement—for love is precisely what he lacks. This becomes apparent not so much from his broken engagement, as from his claim that he is justified. When he asks, "why must she be in the right, and I in the wrong?" the young man expresses precisely the opposite of what, at least according to *Either/Or*'s sermon, characterizes love: the desire to be "always in the wrong" in relation to the beloved. *Repetition* does not go so far as the actualization of love (apart from its references to the story of Job); rather, it offers philosophical grounding for this form of truth, while emphasizing that it can be reached only by a movement beyond philosophy. Faith and love, as the positive content of religious truth, are explored more fully in *Fear and Trembling* and will be discussed extensively in the following chapter. Here, I hope to have clarified the significance of the actualizing movement—the kinesis—that is essential to Kierkegaard's account of subjective, existential truth.

∞

Repetition teaches that the truth involves becoming: the idea is brought into existence. For Kierkegaard, this actualizing movement must be a feature of the communication of truth, as well as of the truth itself. As "a polemic against the truth as knowledge," his texts avoid the direct communication that belongs to representation and attempt instead to bring the truth into being within the reader. This is done in two stages, through the communicative techniques of dramatization and edification. The concept of repetition is dramatized, *brought to life*, in the fictional (or not so fictional!) character of the young man. Edification—which is presented at the end of *Either/Or* as a power of actualization—signifies the "coming into being" of the truth within the existing individual.

In *Repetition* Kierkegaard draws attention to these techniques by thematizing them explicitly.[34] Of course, from our perspective the whole text is a dramatization of the philosophical issues of movement and truth. Within this, Constantin provides a kind of echo of the author's dramatizing power: in his concluding letter to the reader he emphasizes that he has created the character of the young man, "as it were, brought him to birth."[35] In his response to Heiberg, Constantin clarifies his intention to present the category of repetition dramatically:

> Not in a learned manner, still less in a manner so scientific that every teller in our philosophical bank could say "one, two, three," I desire to describe and illustrate psychologically and aesthetically; in the

Greek sense I would let the concept come into being in the individual, in the situation.

Constantin visits the theater during his stay in Berlin, and several pages are devoted to his reflections on dramatic performance and its effect on the audience. Edification can also be seen to be at work within the text, for it is through reading the Book of Job that the young man comes to understand his own situation in terms of repetition. Edification aims to "strengthen the inner being," which reflects the vocabulary of power and inwardness that is used to describe repetition: inspired by Job, the fiancé is strengthened in his struggle against ethics and gains the courage to proclaim himself an exception to moral judgment.

The motif of the theater illustrates the way in which Kierkegaard combines the techniques of dramatization and edification in order to create movement. The idea is actualized in a double way: through being acted out on the text's 'stage,' it has an effect on the reader. The aim is to bring about not an increase in knowledge, but an increase in inwardness. In a sense, the aesthetic form of the text is itself a disguise, for it conceals a hidden *interest* in its effects. In *The Point of View for My Work as an Author*, Kierkegaard claims that even his aesthetic, pseudonymous writings are the work of a religious author, which suggests that a text such as *Repetition* is charged with edifying intent. Constantin reflects this duplicity in his concluding comment that his apparent "indifference to the young man" was part of a deliberate attempt to create a misunderstanding, "in order by this means to bring him out."[36]

Theater is an art form that relies on movement and repetition: the script is not yet theater, for drama—like existential truth—*is* only when it is actualized. The difference between a script and a production is perhaps something like the difference between 'straight philosophy' and Kierkegaard's writing: *Repetition* offers movements, not representation; it takes place within the dimensions of existence, as opposed to ideality. Deleuze's interpretation of Kierkegaard emphasizes this connection between theatricality and movement:

> Kierkegaard [is] among those who bring to philosophy new means of expression . . . Furthermore, in all [his] work, *movement* is at issue . . . [He] wants to put metaphysics in motion, in action, to make it act . . . It is not enough, therefore, to propose a new representation of movement; representation is already mediation. Rather, it is a question of producing within the work a movement capable of affecting the mind outside of all

representations; it is a question of making movement itself a work . . . "I look only at movements" is the language of a director who poses the highest theatrical problem, the problem of a movement which would directly touch the soul, which would be that of the soul.[37]

In *Repetition* Kierkegaard dramatizes inwardness itself: the text's 'stage' is the consciousness of an existing individual. Both the text and the subjectivity that it expresses are centers of power and movement, creative spaces of actualization where the passions, significances, and intensities of existence are unfolded. *Repetition* attempts a kinesis of its own, through this movement reaching beyond philosophy's conceptual "measuring rod" to bring into being *a different kind of truth—a truth that comes from the heart;* the truth of love; the truth as inwardness.

Chapter Six

∞

Fear and Trembling: A Higher Plane

In *Fear and Trembling* as in *Repetition*, the theme of movement pervades the text and helps to illuminate its coherence. This book's pseudonymous author, Johannes de silentio, explores the biblical story of Abraham's journey to Mount Moriah in order to sacrifice his son Isaac, discussing in particular the "movements" of resignation and faith that characterize Abraham's religious existence. While the emphasis in *Repetition* is on an actualizing movement—the transition from ideality to existence—Johannes de silentio seems to be quite preoccupied with movements of elevation and descent. This is not to say that *Fear and Trembling* proposes an alternative movement to repetition: the individual's power for actualization, or kinesis, remains the criterion of truth, and Abraham's movements exemplify the realization of this truth. In this third 1843 text Kierkegaard is concerned to set up a kind of scale of spiritual, existential value; to place Abraham and his faith at the top of this scale; to articulate what is required of the individual who ascends to the highest, religious form of consciousness; and to reveal something of God's transcendent power.

In the preface and epilogue that frame the text, Johannes de silentio invokes a comparison between the world of commerce and the "world of ideas." He complains that his intellectual contemporaries—in other words, Hegelians—set a "low price" on faith, placing it at the bottom of a scale of value that ranks the concept as the highest form of truth. Just as cargoes of produce may be destroyed in order to inflate their price, so some measure needs to be taken in the spiritual world in order to elevate the value of faith. Echoing *Repetition*'s attempt to accomplish a *reversal* of the movement of truth so that the idealizing direction of knowledge is replaced by the actualizing direction of existence, *Fear and Trembling* argues that the relative positions of faith and conceptual thought within the Hegelian system must be reversed: intellectual reflection is relegated to the lowest level of the aesthetic, and faith ascends to a height that properly reflects Abraham's greatness.

The spiritual elevation that characterizes the movement of faith is expressed through the recurring image of a dancer's graceful leap. In a draft title page for *Fear and Trembling*, Kierkegaard uses the pseudonymous name Simon Stylita, "Solo Dancer and Private Individual," and gives the book the subtitle "Movements and Positions."[1] This links the idea of a scale of value consisting of various existential positions (aesthetic, ethical, religious) to the idea that religiousness consists of repeated existential movements, a sequence of leaps: movement is required in order to attain the position of faith, and indeed the position itself is dynamic.

The image of elevation is also a useful expression for *Fear and Trembling*'s relationship to *Repetition*. Kierkegaard published these texts together, and they are companion pieces intended to be read alongside one another: both are concerned with subjective truth—with love—and its conflict with ethics; both oppose Hegelian mediation with an inward, existential movement; both articulate an elevation of consciousness in the hope of effecting such a transformation in the reader. However, *Fear and Trembling* may be distinguished from *Repetition* insofar as the character of Abraham offers a positive paradigm of religious faith. Abraham is, above all, a man who makes a movement: he travels for three days to Mount Moriah, and in his heart, soul, or "inwardness" he makes a leap of faith at every moment along the way. If *Repetition* sets out the criteria for existential truth—*fidelity*, truthfulness to oneself or to another; *actualization*, for the constancy of faith can be attained only through its repeated coming-into-being; and *passion*, the inward, subjective power that effects this movement of actualization—then *Fear and Trembling* presents the fulfillment of these criteria. There can be little doubt that Abraham is existentially "higher" than the fiancé: although they both find themselves in conflict with ethics and facing the loss of a loved one, in the case of Abraham his love and his loss cannot be separated from his relationship to God, and this gives them an absolute significance. More crucially, for Kierkegaard the distinctive mark of faith is the preservation of love within one's finite, earthly existence—and this is precisely what Abraham achieves, and what the young man of *Repetition* fails to achieve. For these reasons, then, *Fear and Trembling* moves beyond *Repetition*. (It would also make sense to read the texts in the opposite order, so that *Repetition* provides philosophical consolidation for Kierkegaard's argument that Abraham's movements take him higher than the ethical sphere. And indeed, *Repetition* picks up where *Fear and Trembling* leaves off: Johannes de silentio concludes his epilogue with a reference to Heraclitus's doctrine of flux and the Eleatic denial of motion, and of course Constantin begins his enquiry into repetition with Diogenes's challenge of this Eleatic thesis.)

As we have seen, the theme of love is important in both *Either/Or* and *Repetition*, but it is in *Fear and Trembling* that love finds its fullest, most powerful expression. (The imagery of elevation resonates here, too: anyone who has been in love will recognize the way in which it raises one above the ordinary level of existence, giving the whole world a heightened significance. Love raises the stakes of life, for the higher value it confers means that there is more to lose. This applies to all kinds of love, including religious love which at once surpasses and elevates the individual through his relationship to God.) The book's title comes from St. Paul's Letter to the Philippians—"work out your own salvation with fear and trembling"—and in a journal entry reflecting on this passage Kierkegaard remarks that love is "the *primus motor* in the Christian life."[2] If existential truth is characterized by repetition, a movement of actualization, then it is love that constitutes the actualizing power. This applies both to God's enduring creation of the world and to the individual's continual actualization of his own life, with all its connections to the lives of others. Christianity emphasizes that the essence of God is love, and that human existence can be a reflection (or a repetition) of this divine activity. Through the story of Abraham, *Fear and Trembling* explores the nature of love and its processes of operation, arguing that love is a "double movement" that realizes two kinds of acceptance: an acceptance of suffering (resignation), and a subsequent acceptance of joy (faith). Resignation helps to actualize the individual's love for God, but faith goes further and actualizes God's love for the individual. Only this faith, this new-found receptivity to God's loving power, accomplishes a transcendent movement.

In this chapter, we will begin by considering the scale of value that Kierkegaard invokes in order to accommodate Abraham's greatness. The notion of passion, of a power for actualization, is crucial to this scale and expresses opposition to the Hegelian "measuring rod," which sets up the concept as the highest standard for truth. As in *Either/Or* and *Repetition*, Kierkegaard's concern here is to recast the relationship between philosophy and existence so that intellectual reflection, far from comprehending the totality of spirit, is incapable of making any movement in the direction of existential truth. We shall then turn to the Kierkegaardian movements of resignation and faith, exploring the ways in which these respond to the experiences of love and suffering. Finally, we will consider how the movement of faith expresses God's transcendent, transforming power, which restores the finite world as a gift to the faithful individual.

∽

Fear and Trembling begins with a comparison between the intellectual world and the commercial world: "not only in the business world but also in the world of ideas, our age stages a real sale."[3] Johannes de silentio suggests that both of these "worlds" are selling their products "at a bargain price," and goes on to introduce the categories of doubt and faith. Kierkegaard's point here is that his contemporaries in the academic world are presuming to reach doubt and faith too soon, without any of the intellectual, emotional, and spiritual expenditure these categories demand:

> Every speculative monitor who conscientiously signals the important trends in modern philosophy, every assistant professor, tutor and student, every rural outsider and tenant incumbent in philosophy is unwilling to stop with doubting everything but must go further . . . They have all made this preliminary movement and presumably so easily that they find it unnecessary to say a word about how . . . how a person is to act in carrying out this enormous task.[4]

The analysis of Abraham that follows aims to emphasize the difficulty of the movement of faith and to explore this question of "how a person is to act" in making such a movement.

In the epilogue Johannes de silentio returns to his claim that the task of faith is underrated in the present age, and once again draws parallels between commercial and spiritual value. Just as cargoes of spices may be sunk into the sea to inflate the price of the remaining produce, so some kind of measure is needed in the world of ideas in order to raise the value of faith. It is clear from the text as a whole that it is Hegelian philosophy, and in particular its principle of mediation, which needs to be "sunk," because this operates a scale of value according to which the greatness of Abraham and of his faith cannot be maintained. Johannes argues that within a system that prioritizes reason and conceptual transparency, faith is relegated to a position of "immediacy," from which one must "go further" in order to attain spiritual elevation:

> Recent philosophy has allowed itself simply to substitute the immediate for "faith . . ." This puts faith in the rather commonplace company of feelings, moods, idiosyncrasies, *vapeurs*, etc. If so, philosophy may be correct in saying that one ought not to stop there. But nothing justifies philosophy in using this language. Faith is preceded by a movement of infinity; only then does faith commence, *nec opinate*, by virtue of the absurd.[5]

As we shall see, it is the "infinite movement" of resignation that fills faith with spiritual value, providing the momentum for elevation.

Johannes de silentio wants to show that Abraham's greatness depends on the recognition of a value, or a form of truth, which is higher than mediation—for according to Hegelian philosophy, Abraham's actions cannot be justified and we must condemn him as a murderer. But what scale of valuation could accommodate Abraham's greatness? Because Johannes does not tell us explicitly, we have to return to the interpretation of truth suggested by *Repetition*. For Kierkegaard, repetition signifies an existential truth belonging to subjectivity, to inwardness. This inwardness is, we recall, constituted by a movement of intensity—by passion. Passion expresses the individual's *power* for actualization; it is a kind of spiritual kinesis. The criterion of truth as repetition is *the capacity to produce a movement*.

This means that, while the Hegelian scale of truth ascends according to increasing intellectual clarity, the Kierkegaardian scale of truth ascends according to increasing subjective intensity, increasing power, increasing freedom. This gives us the progressive movement from aesthetic, to ethical, to religious forms of existence. As we found in *Either/Or*, the aesthete is characterized by his spiritual impotence: he flits between possibilities, but is unable to actualize any of them. The ethical way of life is existentially "higher" insofar as it involves the individual's discovery of his freedom, his capacity for action, and of the real difference between good and evil that makes this action significant. However, these qualities are, for Kierkegaard, limited by the demand of universality that is essential to ethics. Religiousness—the double movement of resignation and faith—expresses the maximum passion, accomplishes the greatest transformation, and is, therefore, the highest truth.

There are various "movements and positions" presented in *Fear and Trembling*, and they may be interpreted in terms of this existential scale of valuation. The role of the pseudonym Johannes de silentio is important in this respect, because his narrative voice helps to establish the relative positions of intellectual reflection, infinite resignation, and faith. Johannes himself occupies an intermediate place on the scale invoked by the text—he is higher than Hegel and lower than Abraham. This position is expressed through his contrasting attitudes toward these two characters: he is dismissive and contemptuous of Hegelian philosophers, "assistant professors," "enterprising abstractors," and "the important trends in modern philosophy," while he regards Abraham with reverence and awe. In other words, Johannes *looks down upon* Hegel and *looks up to* Abraham, and this helps to establish Kierkegaard's new "existentialist," religious scale of value.

Johannes de silentio criticizes Hegelian philosophy, and reflective thinking in general, for being existentially impotent. He emphasizes that *"Every movement of infinity is carried out through passion, and no reflection can produce a movement. This is a continual leap in existence that explains the movement, whereas mediation is a chimera."*[6] (This rather obscure remark is later clarified a little by Johannes Climacus's suggestion that "only when reflection comes to a halt can a beginning be made, and reflection can be halted only by something else, and this something else is quite different from the logical, being a resolution of the will.")[7] Kierkegaard's point is that someone who is engaged in reflection is indifferent to existence, and so detached from it; entering actuality—making a "beginning," or making a movement—requires an act of decision. This represents the transition from a realm of necessity to a realm of freedom; Johannes insists that a genuine movement cannot be "a result of a *dira necessitas*."[8] Here, as in *Either/Or*, the necessity that characterizes the Hegelian dialectic is connected to an inability to make a movement.

Hegelian mediation is also criticized on the grounds that its movement is external, or externalizing, rather than inward: "In Hegelian philosophy, *das Aussere (die Entausserung)* is higher than *das Innere*."[9] This is the case whether the mediation is rational, social, or historical, and Johannes de silentio is concerned to distinguish from each of these spheres the kind of truth he finds in the story of Abraham. Abraham's actions are an offense to reason: to be at once willing to kill Isaac *and* faithful in God's promise to make him the father of a nation simply does not make sense. Abraham's silence expresses the impossibility of social mediation; in his case, society's ethical judgments are themselves a temptation that Abraham resists. Mediation, whether rational or social, requires transparency, the translation of interiority into exteriority:

> In the ethical view of life, it is the task of the single individual to strip himself of the qualification of interiority and to express this in something external... The paradox of faith is that there is an interiority that is incommensurable with exteriority, an interiority that is not identical with the first but is a new interiority.[10]

Johannes also opposes the interpretation of history in terms of mediation and progression that was popular among Hegelians. The idea that a "higher" truth emerges with successive generations is undermined if movements of spiritual actualization take place purely within the individual's inwardness:

> No generation learns the essentially human from the previous one. In this respect, each generation begins primitively, has no task other than what each previous generation had, nor does it advance any further... The essentially human is passion... For example, no generation has learned to love from another... [T]he highest passion in a person is faith, and here no generation begins at any other point than where the previous one did.[11]

The opinion that the modern age is already at an advanced stage in the realization of spirit is, in Kierkegaard's view, not only wrong but potentially detrimental to the process of becoming religious.

In the "Exordium" section of the book, Johannes de silentio introduces Abraham through a nameless character who is passionately interested in the story of the journey to Mount Moriah. Johannes describes how this character's attraction to Abraham develops as he grows up, as he himself goes through life. He hears the story as a child, and

> When he grew older, he read the same story with even greater admiration, for life had fractured what had been united in the pious simplicity of the child. The older he became, the more often his thoughts turned to that story; his enthusiasm for it became greater and greater; and yet he could understand the story less and less.[12]

This man's passion grows in inverse proportion to his understanding, and his self-development is in contrast to the Hegelian movement of increasing conceptual clarity. His appreciation of the significance of Abraham's story certainly deepens, but it does so through lived experience and passionate engagement rather than through rational reflection.

According to the scale of value invoked by this text, and by *Repetition*, Johannes de silentio is positioned above Hegelian philosophy by virtue of his passion. He suggests that distinguishing between what one does and does not understand, and then making "the authentic Socratic movement, the movement of ignorance," requires a certain degree of passion. Johannes demonstrates this discretionary power when he remarks that, while he has understood Hegelian philosophy fairly well, he is unable to comprehend Abraham:

> I am constantly aware of the prodigious paradox that is the content of Abraham's life, I am constantly repelled and, despite all its passion, my thought cannot penetrate it, cannot get ahead by a hairsbreadth. I stretch every muscle to get a perspective, and at the very same instant I become paralyzed.[13]

This recognition of his intellectual limitations—and, indeed, of the limitations of intellectual reflection in general when it comes to appreciating Abraham's greatness—echoes the position that Constantin Constantius reaches by the end of *Repetition*. Just as Constantin realizes that the actualizing movement constituting the truth as repetition is "too transcendent" for him, and consequently "renounces all theorizing," so Johannes emphasizes his inability to understand Abraham and to make the movement of faith. These positions constitute a form of the movement of resignation: as we shall see, resignation expresses the individual's renunciation of claims upon existence—claims based upon an assumption of the world's rational and moral order. In the "Preliminary Expectoration," Johannes states that this order is absent from the "external and visible world." The accomplishment of both pseudonyms is to renounce their intellectual claim upon what they recognize as a transcendent religious movement. In this way they are existentially higher than Hegelian philosophers, who, according to Kierkegaard, delude themselves in presuming to comprehend faith and to have moved beyond it.

Johannes de silentio also resembles Constantin Constantius insofar as, in addition to representing a positive movement beyond philosophical reflection, he functions as a negative indication of an actualizing movement. Just as in *Repetition* Constantin's external movements—his journey to Berlin—contrast with the fiancé's inward movement, so Johannes compares his own movements to those of Abraham:

> For my part, I presumably can describe the movements of faith, but I cannot make them. In learning to go through the motions of swimming, one can be suspended from the ceiling in a harness and then presumably describe the movements, but one is not swimming. In the same way I can describe the movements of faith.[14]

This distinction between describing movements and making movements highlights the importance of actuality—and indeed, Johannes remarks, with regard to movements, that "their relation to actuality . . . is the central issue."[15] Whereas Johannes de silentio, like most of Kierkegaard's narrators, is a commentator on philosophy, psychology, spirituality, and so on, Abraham does not indulge in these kinds of reflections. On the contrary, he offers no explanations, remains silent, and simply acts.

※

The scale of truth invoked by *Fear and Trembling* ascends according to the increasing passion of the individual, and Abraham is at the top of this scale: he is "the greatest of all." But what, exactly, does Kierkegaard mean by passion—by *religious* passion? What gives this kind of passion its depth, and its animating power?

Passion can signify both love and suffering—and this seems particularly resonant in the case of the Passion of Christ. The intimate relationship between love and suffering is one of the most important themes in Kierkegaard's writing, and the examples of suffering that interest him are invariably those caused by the loss of a loved one. Abraham's suffering is due to his love for his son, whom he is asked to sacrifice—and the command to kill Isaac is compelling precisely because of Abraham's love for God. It is clear that the intensity of Abraham's pain as he raises his knife over Isaac's body corresponds to the intensity of his love for his son. This pain is "the highest price" that Abraham could pay for expressing his love for God. In choosing to obey God he is not thereby relativizing his love for Isaac: on the contrary, Abraham's love for God corresponds to what he is prepared to sacrifice for Him, and this love has infinite depth precisely insofar as he gives up *everything*, for Isaac is everything to Abraham. One might imagine that, cast into this situation, Abraham would become paralyzed, unable to make a decision because he lacks a basis upon which to choose between two absolute values. The element that prevents this happening—that allows Abraham to make a choice, and thus to make a movement—is his faith that God loves him. Just as rational criteria are unable to help Abraham decide between two absolutes, so this faith in God's love cannot be grounded by reason. According to rationality, a command that Abraham inflict such tremendous suffering on himself and on Isaac, *and* destroy the future society that Isaac represents, without any gain to anyone, cannot be an expression of love. For Kierkegaard, it is precisely this lack of rational justification that testifies to the greatness of Abraham's faith.

In his account of infinite resignation Johannes de silentio emphasizes the *suffering* that belongs to passion. (The Danish *lidenskab*, "passion," shares a root with the verb *lide*, "to suffer.") Resignation is acceptance of suffering through a renunciation of earthly happiness—such as may come from a loving relationship with another person. This movement is full of pain: "infinite resignation is that shirt mentioned in an old legend. The thread is spun with tears, bleached with tears; the shirt is sewn in tears."[16] Johannes's emphasis on suffering is crucial not only because it signifies his rejection of the Hegelian interpretation of faith in terms of immediacy, and his claim that faith lies on the far side of a great existential struggle (a struggle that infinitely exceeds the difficulties of understanding this or that philosophy) —but also because it avoids any misunderstanding of the familiar Kierkegaardian notion of a "leap of faith." The apparent ease and lightness of this movement is dependent on the individual bearing the full weight of existence. Just as the dancer's graceful elevation can be achieved only after vigorous training to strengthen the muscles, so the individual's elevation to faith—to the enjoyment of *God's* grace—comes after a hard struggle to confront the painful reality of the finite world. The suffering contained in the movement of resignation is preserved within the movement of faith, just as the strength gained through practice is preserved within the dancer's leap.

In Johannes de silentio's account of infinite resignation, we find a gathering of the themes integral to Kierkegaard's interpretation of movement: passion, inwardness, freedom, and love. These elements are also constitutive of faith, although they are transformed *through faith* by becoming expressions of God's activity rather than of the individual's effort. It is love that is central to both resignation and faith; passion, inwardness, and freedom are significant insofar as they are essential to the actualization of love.

The journey to Mount Moriah, and home again, expresses "the double movement in Abraham's soul."[17] Although in a sense the outward journey (a departure from the finite, social world) represents Abraham's resignation of Isaac, and his return home (a return to the finite world) represents his holding on to Isaac through faith, the two aspects of the double movement occur together, repeatedly and reciprocally, each taking place at every moment. Nevertheless, the movement of infinite resignation precedes faith, grounds it and is preserved within it, providing the elevating momentum to the spiritual height—or depth—from which faith operates.

As I have suggested, ascension up the scale of value that is implicit in Kierkegaard's analysis of Abraham occurs through an intensification of passion. This is expressed in Johannes de silentio's movement beyond Hegelian philosophy: through his passionate interest in the story of Abraham, the pseudonym rejects the principle of mediation together with the project of objective conceptual comprehension to which it belongs. The intellect's renunciation of its claims upon existence is a crucial element of resignation—it is the first movement of passion, for "only when reflection comes to a halt can a beginning be made"—but it is not the most significant. The act of will that grounds the intellectual resignation exemplified by Johannes de silentio also accomplishes its movements in relation to the individual's emotional and ethical consciousness. Infinite resignation concerns the individual's claims to happiness and justice within the finite world, as well as the claims of his understanding upon this world.

From a philosophical point of view, these questions of happiness and justice open up the sphere of ethics. Christian doctrine presents the task of reconciling belief in a loving, all-powerful God with the experiences of suffering and injustice that characterize all human existence—and Johannes de silentio raises this issue when he discusses the imperfections of the finite world in the "Preliminary Expectoration." The prevailing philosophical interpretations of Kierkegaard's time—those of Kant and Hegel—approach this ethical question by attempting to preserve and to secure the individual's claims of happiness and justice. Of course, each proceeds very differently: Kant advocates a rational belief in a just God and an immortal soul in order to realize the moral freedom lacking in the phenomenal world, while Hegel proclaims a more concrete reconciliation between the finite world and God. (Hegel's argument, against Kantian philosophy, that this reconciliation is immanent to history is one of the reasons why Kierkegaard is far more vehemently opposed to him than he is to Kant.) Despite these differences, however, both Kant and Hegel establish the self's connection with God *through reason*, so that the claim *upon* God—that human existence *makes sense*, intellectually and morally—is secured as rational. Crucially, for Kierkegaard, this dominion of reason renders the individual's actions as expressions of *necessity*, whether in accordance with the categorical imperative or the principle of mediation.

Resignation approaches the matter differently. Instead of attempting to secure the individual's claims upon existence, Kierkegaard insists that Christianity requires that these claims be renounced. As Johannes de silentio demonstrates in his "Preliminary Expectoration," the incommensurability between the finite world and the spiritual world can be accepted (as, indeed, it is in Kant's philosophy); recognizing that the "eternal divine order" of the spiritual world is lacking in temporal existence, the individual gives up his expectations of earthly happiness. This movement is a process of detachment from the finite world—once the lover renounces his beloved, her finite existence no longer concerns him. The consciousness that once looked outward for its fulfillment and its ethical justification now turns inward; the movement of resignation accomplishes the opening-up of inwardness that we have already encountered in *Repetition*:

> Spiritually speaking, everything is possible, but in the world of the finite there is much that is not possible. This impossibility, however, the knight makes possible by expressing it spiritually, but he expresses it spiritually by waiving his claim to it. The wish which would carry him out into actuality, but has been stranded on impossibility, is now turned inward, but it is not therefore lost, nor is it forgotten.[18]

By this inward movement the individual is reconciled to existence. There is a sense in which this allows him to achieve a kind of repose, a sense of peace: "to find myself and again rest in myself."[19] However, it is important to remember that this peace and rest is preserved only so long as the movement of resignation itself is maintained—and because existence is always becoming, this requires continuous repetition. This means that the individual does not lose his passion; rather, by detaching it from its external object he allows it to fill his whole being. The beloved, and the suffering that her absence brings, are not forgotten: "the knight [of resignation] will recollect everything, but this recollection is precisely the pain."[20]

So, the movement of resignation is an intensification, a deepening of inwardness. The content of this inwardness—or, to put it another way, the power of its movement—is the passion of love and its attendant suffering. The existential value of this movement corresponds to the intensity of the individual's passion: the "highest" movement prior to faith expresses infinite passion. Echoing the fiancé of *Repetition*, Johannes's description of the movement of inwardness envisages a singular point of maximum density, in which the individual "concentrates his whole soul":

> He becomes solitary, and then he undertakes the movement . . . In the first place, the knight will then have the power to concentrate the whole substance of his life and the meaning of actuality into one single desire. If a person lacks this concentration, this focus . . . then he never manages to make the movement . . . In the next place, the knight will have the power to concentrate the conclusion of all his thinking into one act of consciousness. If he lacks this focus . . . he will never find the time to make the movement.[21]

The movement of resignation expresses all the strength, all the power, of the individual: "I continually use my strength in resigning everything . . . I use all my strength in resigning"; "it takes strength and energy and freedom of spirit to make the infinite movement of resignation."[22] This vocabulary of power—which we have already encountered in *Either/Or* and *Repetition*—clarifies the significance of the theme of movement within the 1843 texts.

This brings us to the next essential point about resignation: its freedom. As we have seen, this emphasis on freedom is directed primarily against the necessity that characterizes the Hegelian dialectic. Resignation, because it moves inward, disconnects the individual from precisely those spheres in which mediation is supposed to operate: rationality, history, and society. The opening-up of inwardness that resignation achieves is an expression of the individual's freedom from these external forces. However, this freedom also has a more positive significance, for freedom is essential to love. The knight of infinite resignation "has grasped the deep secret that in loving another person one ought to be sufficient to oneself."[23] Love is a kind of power: it belongs to freedom and can never be the result of a compulsion or a need. As the sermon at the end of *Either/Or* proclaims, "it is in love that you find yourself in freedom."

The movement of resignation enables the individual to actualize his love for God: "what I gain in resignation is my eternal consciousness . . . my eternal consciousness is my love for God."[24] Through acceptance of his suffering, the knight of resignation abandons those claims and expectations that make his relationship to God conditional, as opposed to free. Genuine love is that which expects no return (and as Kierkegaard remarks in his *Works of Love*, love for someone deceased is for this very reason the purest, "most unselfish" kind of love.)[25] The great cost of this movement, however, is the happiness that may be gained from finite love. The freedom achieved through resignation—the freedom that facilitates religious love—is a freedom *from* the temporal, social world; resignation is a "monastic movement."[26] Of course, most knights of resignation continue to live in this world, but they are not at home there:

> Most people live completely absorbed in worldly joys and sorrows; they are benchwarmers who do not take part in the dance. The knights of infinity are ballet dancers and possess elevation. They make the upward movement and come down again . . . but every time they come down, they are unable to assume the posture immediately, they waver for a moment, and this wavering shows that they are aliens in the world.[27]

This expresses the difference, the singularity, that is essential to Kierkegaard's interpretation of truth in terms of inwardness. We have seen how the truth as repetition is opposed to the order of generality that grounds both conceptual understanding and the ethical law. In infinite resignation, the renunciation of claims and expectations upon God represents a departure from generality, for claims are grounded on a logic of rights, of universality (as can be seen in the case of judicial claims). Claims are made on the basis of belonging to a genus, rather than on the basis of individuality; we speak of "human rights" or "animal rights." One might expect justice and happiness from God *as His creature*, or perhaps even *as a Christian*. In renouncing this form of self-understanding, the individual makes possible his love for God—for this love must be an expression of singularity, of subjectivity. I love not insofar as I am subject to a law but, on the contrary, insofar as I am free.[28] The full significance of this singularity emerges in the movement of faith; resignation prepares for this by departing, in inwardness, from the order of generality.[29]

Infinite resignation is the greatest movement that an individual is capable of making, demanding *all* his effort, strength, and courage. Through this inward concentration of power, of passion, the knight of resignation becomes fully individualized, for he distinguishes himself from the world and from everything within it: Johannes de silentio emphasizes that "I make this movement all by myself."[30] Although this self-sufficiency, this freedom, is an essential requirement for love, it also constitutes the limitation of the movement of infinite resignation. If it seems contradictory to speak of the limits of an infinite movement, then this is precisely the point: the transition from resignation to an even greater movement is paradoxical, transgressing the boundaries of the understanding.

Infinite resignation is the greatest movement possible *within immanence*.[31] Of all the existential movements it is possible to make—of all the decisions it is possible to take—this is the most difficult and requires the most courage. This explains the significance of the *fear and trembling* that resounds through the religious movement: Johannes de silentio's upward glance to Abraham expresses awe and terror as well as admiration. For the knight of resignation, the fear inspired by existence, by becoming—the constant threat of pain and loss symbolized by "the sword hanging over the beloved's head"—remains incommensurable with the idea of God. Earthly happiness must be given up in order to gain the peace in the soul needed for religious love. There is some sense in which this contact with the eternal is suspended above the continual motion of actuality: although the individual's love for God expresses a movement of actualization, the "eternal being" who is the object of this love seems rather static, ideal, devoid of activity. For Johannes de silentio, "that God is love" is a *thought* that is sometimes present to him and sometimes absent, and because it is merely ideal this thought has no power to change the finite world: "to me God's love, in both the direct and the converse sense, is incommensurable with the whole of actuality." This attitude falls short of faith, for it does not recognize transcendence, does not permit God to have any power. As Johannes admits, "I do not have faith; this courage I lack . . . I do not trouble God with my little troubles, details do not concern me; I gaze only at my love and keep its virgin flame pure and clear."[32] The "little troubles," the "details" that are the content of finitude, are flooded with significance by the movement of faith. This is the paradoxical elevation—the elevation of the individual's finite existence—which distinguishes Abraham and places him beyond the achievement of resignation. Abraham is "higher" than the knight of resignation by virtue of his *descent*, his return to finitude, his movement back "down to earth." The renunciation of the world is at once the movement of resignation and its limit.

∞

We have learned from *Repetition* that inward movement is an expression of power, of self-actualization, and that this is for Kierkegaard the criterion of truth. We have also learned that this kind of truth, or truthfulness, belongs to love and its fidelity, rather than to knowledge. In *Fear and Trembling*, this movement is dramatized in Abraham's journey: "What did Abraham achieve? He remained true to his love."[33] Both of these texts are concerned above all with transcendent movements. If a movement is an expression of power, then a transcendent movement is an expression of God's power, *an actualization of God's love*. From the perspective of the existing individual, to make a transcendent movement is to receive God's loving power, to recognize and to submit to it as the source of his finite, earthly life—and thus both Job and Abraham exemplify this movement, whether it is labeled "repetition" or "faith."

In contrast to the thought "that God is love" described by Johannes de silentio, faith is the belief that *God loves me*. This belief is synonymous with acceptance of God's love; in the movement of faith, inwardness opens itself up to God. While in resignation this opening and acceptance—which are *constitutive of love*—involve detachment from the finite world, in faith a new kind of love is actualized by acceptance *of the finite* as a gift from God. Having been fully "opened up" in the movement of resignation—or, in other words, having reached the maximal intensity of its power, its passion—inwardness is then *transformed* through faith. Once it has risen to the level of the paradoxical, the soul accomplishes its final, highest movement absurdly, unexpectedly; one could say that it *turns inside out*, turns from immanence to transcendence. This is just a rather abstract way of describing the fundamental shift of consciousness that is expressed in faith: "he who loves God without faith reflects upon himself; he who loves God in faith reflects upon God."[34]

Although resignation is the greatest expression of the individual's strength, concentrated in his love for God, faith goes even further in realizing God's love for the individual. The movements of resignation and faith in this sense go in opposite directions, of giving and receiving, although they are connected (a double movement, rather than two separate movements) insofar as giving makes receiving possible. Resignation gives away the finite world in order to give love to the eternal being; faith receives God's love, and in so doing also receives the finite world as His gift. This receiving demands a different courage to that demonstrated by the knight of infinite resignation, "a paradoxical and humble courage," by virtue of "the great mystery that it is far more difficult to receive than to give."[35] It is difficult for the individual to receive God's love because the threat of suffering and loss remains, since it is integral to finitude. Thus Johannes de silentio admires above all the knight of faith: "every moment to see the sword hanging over the beloved's head, and yet not to find rest in the pain of resignation but to find joy by virtue of the absurd—this is wonderful. The person who does this is great, the only great one."[36] In faith, the incommensurability between God's love and the finite world is not dissolved—and this is accentuated by Johannes's description of the religious movement as a "leap."

What kind of a movement is a leap?[37] Most obviously, it is a movement from one place, or one point, to another, and implies that these two points are unconnected—for if there were a path between them, it would be possible to walk the distance and there would be no need for a leap. One of Kierkegaard's examples of a leap is the transition from reflective thinking to existence, which involves "a radical breach."[38] The leap is a movement that arises from difference—just as freedom of choice is grounded by either/or—and, as such, it is opposed to Hegelian mediation. For Kierkegaard, mediation represents precisely the "path" between two points that renders their difference superficial.

The distinction between Kierkegaard's leap and Hegelian mediation becomes clearer when we consider another feature of the leap: its individuality. As the image of the dancer suggests, a leaping movement expresses the energy of a particular individual. Mediation, on the other hand, is an impersonal procedure of thinking, and although it requires some sort of effort it operates through a law of necessity that is indifferent to the existing individual. As we might by now expect, the dynamic power expressed through Kierkegaard's leap constitutes the *freedom* of this movement: "the leap is . . . essentially at home in the realm of freedom"; "the leap is the category of decision," and "all forms of instigation or impulsion constitute precisely an obstacle to making the leap in reality."[39]

The difference or incommensurability that requires the leap of faith is that between temporality and eternity. Johannes de silentio alludes to this in his remark that "dying is one of the greatest leaps."[40] While resignation finds rest in the disjunction between eternity and temporality by prioritizing the eternal, faith returns to the finite world: "Temporality, finitude—that is what it is all about."[41] (Johannes Climacus echoes this: "Leaping means to belong essentially to the earth and to respect the law of gravity so that the leap is merely momentary," ascending only in order to descend again.)[42] Because they are incommensurable, eternity and the finite world are held together in tension, and this provides the momentum needed for a leap: in the movement of faith, "the paradox . . . constitutes the tension of its inwardness." This spiritual tension seems to correspond to passion: "Passion is the very tension in the contradiction," "the highest pitch of subjectivity" in which one is "closest to being in two places at the same time."[43] The knight of faith believes, purely on the strength of the absurd, that the temporal world is a manifestation of God's eternal, unchanging love. This belief, as I have already suggested, means receiving one's finite existence as a gift from God: "If exchange is the criterion of generality, theft and gift are those of repetition."[44] The individuality or singularity that characterizes the leap emerges here: the gift of love is always *for me*; God loves not merely the world in general but *my* existence in particular, in all its details: "faith is convinced that God is concerned about the smallest things."[45] (Indeed, the same is true of death, another Kierkegaardian leap; death as a principle of individuation is explored in Heidegger's *Being and Time* and is revisited in Derrida's *The Gift of Death*.) The transcendent movement involved in God's giving the finite world as a gift accomplishes a movement between eternity and temporality in which the integrity of each is preserved—and as the *Philosophical Fragments* suggests, this paradoxical relationship is exemplified above all in the Christian incarnation.

In making the movement of faith, the individual achieves the greatest elevation; this leap is the smoothest, most *graceful* transition between heaven and earth. The elevation to transcendence that occurs in faith is the elevation of one's existence as being loved by God, as receiving God's grace.[46] If Kierkegaard's insistence on both freedom and transcendence seems problematic, his emphasis on love helps to clarify this. Freedom and transcendence are both forms of power: freedom signifies human power and transcendence signifies divine power. Both of these are essential for the actualization of a loving relationship between God and the individual; although God's power is infinitely greater than man's, the individual can reciprocate God's love only if he is free.[47] Love requires a purely inward, spiritual kind of freedom unaffected by the causal and logical laws that determine other spheres of existence.

The way in which receiving presupposes giving suggests a certain ambiguity with regard to the objectivity of God—for there are two kinds of giving involved here: God's gift and the individual's renunciation. The transcendence of the former movement accentuates Kierkegaard's conviction of the reality or objectivity of God: his insistence on the subjectivity of faith need not imply concession to a "non-realist" interpretation of Christianity (although it may certainly inspire such a view, which would emphasize the individual's movement of giving away).[48] Faith is a response to God, through which the finite world *really does become* the manifestation of God's love. The knight of faith is the happiest man, he is blessed. Again, Kierkegaard insists that for the Christian this joy requires a God with the power of blessing.

This phrase, "the power of blessing," expresses the crux of the issues raised in this reading of *Fear and Trembling*. Of course, our focus on movement has led to an emphasis on the theme of power, but it should also be kept in view that the text is profoundly engaged with questions of happiness—it is for this reason that Johannes de silentio seems to be so preoccupied with stories of suffering. The scale of existential truth, of greatness, which Kierkegaard invokes in order to demonstrate the significance of Abraham's actions, expresses degrees of happiness alongside degrees of power. The characters belonging to the lowest existential level of the aesthetic—notably, abstract thinkers and students of philosophy—are melancholy in their impotence; at the top of the scale, "the peak upon which Abraham stands," the individual finds both transcendent power and earthly joy: "the knight of faith is the only happy man, the heir to the finite," and "he finds pleasure in everything."[49] From the perspective of infinite resignation, between these two extremes, Johannes de silentio understands that "I am happy and satisfied, but my joy is not the joy of faith, and by comparison with that, it is unhappy."[50] For Kierkegaard, the happiness enjoyed by the knight of faith is beyond reason, by virtue of the absurd, and grounded by a transcendent power. It belongs to the highest, most spiritually pure form of human existence, but it is also rooted firmly in finitude.

It is interesting to note that Kierkegaard is not the only thinker who emphasizes this connection between power and happiness. Two of the greatest philosophers of power, Spinoza and Nietzsche, understand joy as the expression of an increase in the individual's existential power. For Spinoza, joy is "that passion by which the mind passes to a greater perfection . . . When I say that someone passes from a lesser to a greater perfection . . . we conceive that his power of acting . . . is increased."[51] When Nietzsche, toward the end of his career, was crystallizing his thoughts on power (and as he faced increasing mental and physical suffering), he wrote:

> *To feel stronger*—or in other words, joy—always presupposes a comparison (but not necessarily with others, but with oneself in the midst of a state of growth and without one's first *knowing* in how far one is making the comparisons—).
>
> . . . it is notably enlightening to posit *power* in place of individual "happiness" (after which every living thing is supposed to be striving): "there is a striving for power, for an increase of power";—pleasure is only a symptom of the feeling of power attained, a consciousness of difference.[52]

What Nietzsche describes here signifies, like Kierkegaard's leap, an inward motion of consciousness that is grounded on difference and that expresses power. And as in the re-valuation of existential truth that is at work in each of Kierkegaard's 1843 texts, this repeated expression of power is experienced by the individual as happiness. Of course, Kierkegaard's emphasis is on the claim that *for the Christian* true happiness involves receptivity to God's power, whereas both Spinoza and Nietzsche clearly distinguish their philosophies from Christian teaching and insist on immanence. Their interpretations of happiness are consequently quite different from Kierkegaard's: Spinoza describes the joy and blessedness of complete self-understanding, whilst Nietzsche admires the high-spirited self-affirmation of creative individuals. But insofar as happiness is happiness, regardless of one's religious or philosophical position, it would be enlightening to explore this correspondence between power (or movement) and joy that is common to all three thinkers. Perhaps, in the end, there may be philosophical as well as religious justification for the view that Abraham is great simply by virtue of his happiness.

Part Three

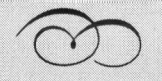

Chapter Seven

Becoming a Christian

Our readings of Kierkegaard's three 1843 texts have brought to light many variations on the theme of movement: metaphors of leaping, dancing, swimming, and sailing; characters who travel, step forward, and pace back and forth; philosophical discussions of kinesis, mediation, and repetition; and reflections on the communicative processes of dramatization and edification. The significance of movement has many layers and involves several rich but rather difficult concepts, such as inwardness, faith, and transcendence, but whenever the theme appears it announces the coherence of each text, and of Kierkegaard's thought as it develops during 1843. We might say, more simply, that movement here means becoming, and *reaching beyond*. For Kierkegaard movement is, in a sense, something unthinkable: it is not a concept but a theme that opposes intellectual reflection and "the truth as knowledge;" that reaches beyond thought, trying to transcend it. The progression from aesthetic to ethical to religious forms of existence is the deepening, intensifying movement of inwardness itself: the Kierkegaardian "stages" or "spheres" are not external but *internal to one another*, connected by an internalizing movement. These existential "spheres" signify degrees of power, which correspond to degrees of happiness.

In *Either/Or* we find that the ability to move distinguishes the ethical individual from the aesthete. Becoming ethical means facing the future and projecting forth into it, whereas the aesthetic consciousness remains static, impotent, gripped by the necessity of the past. Here, making movements means making decisions and commitments: discriminating between possibilities, and actualizing those chosen. Movement requires a recognition of real difference—either/or. This difference is the key to freedom. The sermon at the end of the book explores these issues of difference and freedom in a religious context: the individual's relationship to God is characterized by a profound difference, and freedom is significant insofar as it is essential to love.

Repetition begins with a discussion of various philosophical accounts of movement: the Eleatics' denial of motion, Aristotle's kinesis, Platonic recollection, Hegelian mediation, and the "new category" of repetition. Then an intellectual takes a trip to Berlin, and a young fiancé struggles with changes occurring within him and in his relationships to others. At both of these levels of the text—the philosophical and the dramatic—there is an opposition between idealizing movements and actualizing movements. Constantin Constantius, like the processes of recollection and mediation, seeks the truth as idea, whereas repetition signifies a form of truth that actually requires the movement of becoming. This movement is also the intensification and expansion (deepening) of inwardness, which at once asserts the individual's freedom and distinguishes him from the external, social world. This means that repetition exceeds the sphere of ethics as well as that of knowledge: this kind of movement "is always a transcendence."

Fear and Trembling presents movements expressive of religious faith—Abraham's journey to Mount Moriah, and the graceful leap of the knight of faith. Such movements require a particular kind of power: the power of love that flows between God and the individual in the form of a gift given and received. Faith reveals God's love as the source of all finite things, as the actualizing power that grounds existence. God, then, is the hidden inwardness of beings, and the task of faith is to become receptive, to open up the self to His loving power.

We find in Kierkegaard's writing an interest in movements of going beyond, of transcending. (Just as being and becoming are not things or states of things, but movements, so transcendence signifies something active and dynamic.) Heidegger once remarked that every great thinker pursues a single thought, and if we were to try to identify Kierkegaard's then the theme of movement might provide a clue. It certainly highlights a unity within Kierkegaard's authorship, for both his pseudonymous and his religious writings of 1843 are concerned with "the task of becoming a Christian." This coheres with Kierkegaard's own retrospective view that his "whole literary production" possesses the "integral coherence" and "comprehensiveness" of a single project: "to *make people aware* of the essentially Christian."[1] One of the differences between the two kinds of publication is that in the pseudonymous or "aesthetic" literature the orientation toward Christianity remains implicit (except in the sermon at the end of *Either/Or*), whereas the religious discourses make their edifying intentions very clear.

If we turn to the nine "upbuilding" discourses that Kierkegaard published under his own name during 1843, we find that they share those preoccupations that are articulated by the theme of movement in *Either/Or*, *Repetition*, and *Fear and Trembling*. Although this is not the place to attempt a discussion that could do justice to these religious discourses, we can explore some of the ways in which they cohere with, and illuminate, our three pseudonymous texts.

Kierkegaard's first pair of edifying discourses, *The Expectancy of Faith* and *Every Good and Every Perfect Gift Is from Above*, appeared on May 16, three months after *Either/Or*. In October, on the same day as *Fear and Trembling* and *Repetition*, Kierkegaard published *Three Upbuilding Discourses*—two on *Love Will Hide a Multitude of Sins* and one on *Strengthening in the Inner Being*. These were followed in December by *Four Upbuilding Discourses*—two more on *Every Good and Every Perfect Gift Is from Above*; *The Lord Gave, and the Lord Took Away: Blessed Be the Name of the Lord*; and *To Gain One's Soul in Patience*. Kierkegaard introduces each of these books of discourses with a preface that reflects on his relationship as an author to his reader (who is always singular). At the beginning of the May discourses he describes his hope for the life of his "little book," which is "in a figurative sense starting a journey":

> I saw how it wended its way down solitary paths or walked solitary on public roads. After a few little mistakes, through being deceived by a fleeting resemblance, it finally met that single individual whom I with joy and gratitude call *my* reader, that single individual it is seeking, to whom, so to speak, it stretches out its arms.[2]

Alternatively, Kierkegaard adds, "in as much as in being published it actually remains quiet without moving from the spot," he envisages a reader who seeks out the book, like an attentive bird who "suddenly noticed it, flew down to it, picked it, and took it home." The two other prefaces repeat this vision of the book wandering out to meet its reader; the second also advises that the discourses be read aloud, and the third emphasizes the author's wish for a receptive reader, "who in receiving the book does for it by himself and by his acceptance what the temple box by itself did for the widow's mite: sanctifies the gift, and turns it into much."[3]

Taken as a whole, these nine discourses meditate on themes that we have already discovered in the three pseudonymous texts. They express an interpretation of human existence in terms of inwardness, and indeed they address the reader's soul. Kierkegaard remarks in *To Gain One's Soul in Patience* that "the internal is, after all, in its universal expression, the soul," and the discourse on *Strengthening in the Inner Being* in particular emphasizes his focus on inwardness. As we have seen, inwardness is a movement—a repetition—and in the case of the religious individual this movement has the quality of receptivity as well as passionate activity. The edifying discourses also share the pseudonymous authorship's "polemic against the truth as knowledge," and some explicitly propose in place of knowledge a form of truth belonging to love. And, probably most importantly, they emphasize the themes of power and transcendence: they understand (or decline to understand!) the individual as a center of power, and God as the source of all power. Power means becoming, the emergence of something new, a reaching beyond, and the Christian scriptures reveal as the origin of these movements a *loving* power. This view is well illustrated by the text that is chosen for three of the 1843 discourses—the Letter of James, chapter one, verses 17-22—a passage that is so significant for Kierkegaard, and in any case so beautiful, that it is worth presenting in full:

> Every good and every perfect gift is from above and comes down from the Father of lights, with whom there is no change or shadow of variation. According to his own counsel, he brought us forth by the word of truth, that we should be a first fruit of his creation. Therefore, my beloved brethren, let every man be quick to hear, slow to speak, slow to anger, because a man's anger does not work what is righteous before God. Therefore put away all filthiness and all remnants of wickedness and receive with meekness the word that is implanted in you and that is so powerful for making your souls blessed.

The Letter of James was Kierkegaard's favorite biblical text, and after 1843 he often returns to it in both his religious and pseudonymous writings. This Letter is rather an unusual choice for a Danish Christian, for its insistence that faith is insufficient without good works usually confines it to the margins of the Lutheran tradition.[4] However, as we shall see the above passage contains some of the ideas most essential to Kierkegaard's authorship—ideas that have since inspired Protestant theology, and perhaps even seem in some way to epitomize it.

A prominent theme in the Letter of James is the apostle's insistence that the Word must become a deed. It is not enough simply to listen to and reflect on the truth that Jesus teaches and embodies: receiving the Word fully involves acting upon it, for this kind of truth *is* only when it is actualized. The one who properly accepts the divine Word is quick to hear, slow to speak—"Indeed, what is there for him to say? Ultimately, he will not even say with David: Hasten, O Lord, to speak! but will say to his own soul: Hasten, oh, hasten to listen!"[5] In this discourse on *Every Good and Every Perfect Gift Is from Above*, Kierkegaard describes the edifying effect that Jesus' teachings have on the receptive individual: they "raise him up and strengthen him"; they are "words of power" for they "make his soul blessed." The movement of receptivity, of turning toward God, involves the individual's acceptance that he is not self-sufficient, "that human beings are not capable of giving good gifts," that even though a father's love is a reflection of God's love it "is still never the same as God's, never so strong, never so inward, and therefore is not capable of doing what God's love is capable of doing, which in the power of its love is almighty."[6]

This emphasis on putting the truth into practice, and on our dependence upon God, is connected to Kierkegaard's claim that "the truth as knowledge" is inadequate. In *To Gain One's Soul in Patience* Kierkegaard suggests (again with reference to James) that "all knowing that is unrelated to a gaining is incomplete and deficient, in as much as a person still does not know how he becomes." Knowledge seems here to be associated with worldliness and self-assertion—perhaps with assistant professors who wish to be admired for their conquest of the truth—and these are forces that cling to the soul and ensnare it, or rather that the soul blindly tethers itself to. The individual gains his soul only by giving himself up to God:

> In patience, the soul comes to terms with all its possessors, with the life of the world in that it sufferingly gains itself from it, with God in that it sufferingly accepts itself from him . . . The person who wants to gain his soul in patience knows that his soul does not belong to him, that there is a power from which he must gain it, a power by whom he must gain it, and that he must gain it himself.[7]

Here again we find that the individual is a center of power, and that God is the source of all power, "in whom you live, move, and have your being."[8] It is only in inwardness that one discovers that God is the source of existence—for inwardness *is* this discovery, this unconcealing movement, this becoming of truth. Kierkegaard emphasizes that repetition is needed to sustain this movement over time: gaining one's soul in patience suggests "a quiet but unflagging activity," for "the whole process of gaining . . . is all a repetition." We find again an interpretation of inwardness as an intensifying movement, in which "the soul inclosing spins itself."[9]

Kierkegaard's discourse on *Strengthening in the Inner Being* develops the themes of inwardness and power. This discourse begins by reflecting on Paul's situation as a prisoner in Rome when he wrote his Letter to the Ephesians: his external confinement contrasts with his spiritual freedom, his inner power. Kierkegaard suggests that Paul's inwardness has a transforming strength—"he had the power of miracle . . . To transform hardships into the witness for the truth of a teaching . . . to transform the lost cause into a matter of honor"—that has its source in God's love. "What gave Paul the power for this? . . . he was mightily strengthened by God's spirit in his inner being."[10] Kierkegaard goes on to distinguish between two ways of relating to the world: through knowledge, and through a subjective, passionate "concern" with questions of meaning. As long as he is pursuing knowledge, Kierkegaard argues, the individual "is indifferent to the world and this world is indifferent through his knowledge of it." In other words, "the truth as knowledge" brings to light a valueless, meaningless world—knowledge leads to nihilism. When concern for meaning "awakens in his soul" the individual finds that he requires a form of truth that goes beyond knowledge, that has some actualizing power: "This concern . . . craves another kind of knowledge, a knowledge that does not remain as knowledge for a single moment but is transformed into action the moment it is possessed, since otherwise it is not possessed." Inwardness "craves" the truth as repetition. Kierkegaard emphasizes that movement is essential to this kind of truth, suggesting that inwardness relies on becoming and renewal:

> At no point does this concern cease; the knowledge gained is not an indifferent sort of knowledge. For example, if a person were to have in mind deciding this matter once and for all and then being finished with it, so to speak, the inner being would only be stillborn, and would vanish again.[11]

The task of becoming a Christian involves a repeated relationship to God. The soul sustains itself, preserves its freedom, by drawing on the source of its power. Kierkegaard makes this clear at the end of the discourse:

> Blessed is the person who, even though in his life he made the mistake of taking the outer instead of the inner, even though his soul in many

ways was ensnared by the world, yet was again renewed in the inner being by turning back to his God, strengthened in the inner being.[12]

This echoes Johannes de silentio's remark that "in Hegelian philosophy the outer is higher than the inner": even this religious discourse, supposedly addressed to the simpler man, offers a challenge to Hegel's followers.

The two discourses on *Love Will Hide a Multitude of Sins* are also interesting in the present context because, like the pseudonymous texts, they propose love as an alternative to knowledge. Becoming a Christian requires a form of truth that belongs to inwardness and has actualizing power; in these discourses Kierkegaard presents love as a power of revelation and concealment. Here again he argues that, in contrast to the indifference of knowledge, this kind of truth is rooted in the individual's passionate concern:

> The more the object of observation belongs to the world of the spirit, the more important is the way [the observer] himself is constituted in his innermost nature, because everything spiritual is appropriated in freedom; but what is appropriated in freedom is also brought forth. The difference, then, is not in the external but in the internal . . . A person's inner being, then, determines what he discovers and what he hides.[13]

Here truth is interpreted as a kind of vision, a way of seeing things that illuminates them from a particular perspective: "when love lives in the heart, the eye has the power to love forth the good in the impure." This kind of truth is capable of transforming its object as it reveals it. Once more Kierkegaard insists that, despite the importance of the individual's freedom, the creative force of love has a transcendent source: "there is a power from above that translates evil into good—it is the love that hides a multitude of sins."[14] *Either/Or*, *Repetition*, and *Fear and Trembling* all articulate, in a very complicated and roundabout way, what I have described as 'a form of truth belonging to love.' From the perspective of Christianity, one need merely say that God is love, God is truth, or that Jesus is the way, the truth, and the life.

∽

In these 1843 discourses, then, we find an exploration of the soul that often corresponds to the interpretation of religious existence articulated by the theme of movement in Kierkegaard's pseudonymous texts. The task of becoming a Christian provides a unifying perspective from which to approach the questions of communication provoked by the authorship as a whole (although here our focus remains on the books published in 1843). When we analyze the account of truth in terms of movement offered by the pseudonymous texts, we can identify three cohesive forms of movement: intensification, elevation, and edification. These are all actualizing movements, and they are all directed toward the task of Christianity. Each suggests a vertical axis, a connection between earth and heaven. This axis traditionally expresses the ontology or the worldview of Christianity, and indeed of monotheism more generally: it describes the individual's relationship to God, whether as descending from Him as His creature; as falling away from Him in sin; or as ascending toward him in faith—and it describes the passage of God's grace bestowed upon every being.[15] Intensification signifies the concentration of this vertical axis to a single point, to the soul that constitutes every individual's singularity. This is the closest we can get to a literal description of a movement that is not spatial, of a movement on the spot. Elevation suggests an upward movement, "consciousness raised to the second power," as a metaphor for the spiritual strengthening accomplished through inward intensification. Edifying or upbuilding is, in turn, a metaphor for spiritual elevation, implying the construction and consolidation of the soul through its relationship to God.

Kierkegaard's edifying discourses aim to construct and to consolidate the inward self. As we know, this inwardness 'is' only when it is actualized by the existing individual who Kierkegaard addresses as his reader. This basic intention is shared by the pseudonymous texts; the principal difference is that these texts address a specific type of reader—an intellectual. For such a reader, Christian upbuilding can take place only after demolishing an edifice that already shapes and contains his consciousness: the philosophical System or, more generally, the project of knowledge. Again, Kierkegaard's own reflections on his authorship echo this interpretation of his communicative task. When he presents his well-known distinction between the "direct" approach of the religious discourses and the "indirect" techniques of the pseudonymous books, he suggests that "in relation to pure receptivity, like the empty jar that is to be filled, *direct* communication is appropriate, but when illusion is involved, consequently something that must first be removed, direct communication is inappropriate."[16] Here Kierkegaard describes his pseudonymous writing as "maieutic," meaning a movement that "lies in the relation between the aesthetic productivity as the beginning and the religious as the *telos*."

To say that all of Kierkegaard's work shares this communicative telos is also to suggest that the pseudonymous texts are, eventually, edifying; that they attempt to uncover a capacity for the truth as inwardness within the reader. This raises interesting questions when we consider that Kierkegaard understood his edifying writing as accomplishing *his own* religious education: "I am not a teacher but a learner."[17] Should this be applied to the pseudonymous works too? And if so, is their task of demolition directed to Kierkegaard's own intellectual pretensions as well as to those of his Hegelian contemporaries? It seems that the very personal significance of Kierkegaard's work lies in his relationship to philosophical reflection, and to academia, as well as his more widely discussed relationships with Regine and his father. Like both these pivotal figures, philosophy caused profound inward conflict for Kierkegaard, and the movement from an aesthetic consciousness to religious faith may be what he desired to accomplish himself—a desire played out again and again under various disguises. Reading the 1843 texts, I get a sense that their vocabulary of power and weakness expresses something integral to Kierkegaard's awareness of himself—he would surely be quick to acknowledge that affirmations of faith, strength, and courage have their source in experiences of doubt, fragility, and fear. As we saw in part 1, movement had a psychological significance for Kierkegaard, for at times he complained of lacking existential power: he felt trapped in reflection and in academia, and he lamented his "dreadful still life." He was unable to marry Regine. These emotional themes resonate through the authorship alongside the philosophical and spiritual meanings of movement, propelling Kierkegaard's attempt to uncover, to communicate, and to actualize a *truthful* (and also truly happy) life, capable of motion. As *self*-communication, Kierkegaard's writing is "soul searching"—as we might expect when we consider that he tells us to treat the Bible as a mirror: his books are at once interpretations of the scriptures and interpretations of himself.

Here we have a discovery of the self, of subjectivity. For Kierkegaard, becoming and repetition are the basic elements of the self and must therefore be the categories of a philosophy of existence, of spirituality, of religion. What is the self but movements and positions? Because he or she is continually becoming, the self's positions (like a dancer's) have to be dynamic. Kierkegaard's philosophical originality lies in his substitution of individuals for concepts, so that the relationships between these distinct positions are personal rather than logical and ideal. This is what the pseudonyms and characters of the aesthetic writings accomplish: they are positions who relate to one another humanly, subjectively, which is to say that they are capable of love and loss. The soul, like the world and like

God, is a sphere of relationships, of affective connections between beings, or rather between moments of becoming. Kierkegaard's writing dramatizes inwardness, simply because it cannot be adequately expressed through concepts. The personalities who appear in his pseudonymous texts are aspects, moments or positions of Kierkegaard's inwardness (for who else's could they be?). Just as God is the hidden inwardness of the self, so Kierkegaard is the hidden inwardness of his writing, hiding even as he reveals himself, asserting his absence even as his words repeat themselves to each new reader.

∽

The movement from the aesthetic sphere toward religious inwardness, from philosophy to faith, suggests a trajectory to follow in reading Kierkegaard's later publications. I hope that the present interpretation of the 1843 texts helps us, in the first place, to become more aware of and attentive to the movements that recur throughout Kierkegaard's writing—and then to contextualize these movements in terms of the task of becoming a Christian, and in terms of an attempt to articulate the kind of truth that belongs to religious faith. The way Kierkegaard uses the theme of movement to undermine Hegelian philosophy; the connections between his polemic and the debates surrounding mediation and contradiction in the 1830s; the influence of Aristotle; and the personal, emotional significance of movement that emerges from a biographical perspective, all continue to illuminate the authorship after 1843.

Aristotle's interpretation of kinesis as the transition from potentiality to actuality remains central to Kierkegaard's more philosophical explorations of Christianity. In 1844 he began to study Trendelenburg, who uses Aristotle's modal categories to criticize Hegelian logic, and the *Philosophical Fragments* demonstrates a continuing fascination with kinesis. In this text, Johannes Climacus—whose name suggests a ladder, to be used for ascending and descending movements—starts with a discussion of the Platonic doctrine of knowledge, and emphasizes the immanence of this model of truth. In recollection, "the Truth in which I rest was in me, and came to light through myself," and a teacher such as Socrates plays the role of a midwife. Climacus then describes a different kind of movement from ignorance to truth: "a change takes place within [the individual] like the change from non-being to being . . . this transition we call birth."[18] In the book's "Interlude" Climacus examines this "coming-into-existence kind of change (*kinesis*)," and suggests that it is a transition from not existing to existing, a change in being rather than in essence. "The change involved in coming into existence is actuality, the transition takes place with freedom. No coming into existence is necessary."[19] Here Kierkegaard quite explicitly draws on Aristotelian categories in opposition to the Hegelian movement of mediation and at the same time moves toward an interpretation of truth that coheres with Christian teachings.

In Climacus's discussion of the Incarnation the theme of movement is especially striking. The pseudonym raises the question, "what could move God to make his appearance?," throws in a reference to Aristotle's definition of God as an unmoved mover (*akinesis panta kinei*), and concludes that God becomes a human being because He is moved by love.[20] In contrast with the teacher of knowledge (the Socratic midwife), the teacher—and the teaching—of the Incarnation possesses *actualizing power*:

> When the God becomes a Teacher, his love cannot be merely seconding and assisting, but is creative, giving a new being to the learner, or as we have called him, the man born anew; by which designation we signify the transition from non-being to being.[21]

Johannes Climacus repeatedly emphasizes man's lack of self-sufficiency—here he adds that "the Truth then is that the learner owes the teacher everything." In the *Philosophical Fragments* the polemic against the truth as knowledge that develops in the 1843 texts is applied more directly to Christianity: God is the Unknown, "the limit to which Reason repeatedly comes, and in so far, substituting a static form of conception for the dynamic, it is difference, the absolutely different." In the light of our exploration of *Either/Or*, *Repetition*, and *Fear and Trembling*, even this very brief discussion of Climacus's first project helps to illuminate the coherence of a complex and apparently fragmented text.

Kierkegaard's interpretation of sin also draws on the theme of movement. He published *The Concept of Anxiety* a few days after *Philosophical Fragments* in June 1844, and here he once more approaches Christian teachings from the perspective of the question of becoming—how did the first sin come into the world? how did Adam make the transition from innocence to sin? The puzzle that these questions pose for theologians is analogous to that which confronted the pre-Socratics with respect to natural motion. For a Christian, though, God's goodness and power are at stake—for where did Adam acquire the capacity for sin, if not from God? As we might by now expect, Kierkegaard's solution to this problem of becoming is inspired by Aristotle: he suggests that we understand

Adam's sin in terms of the transition from possibility to actuality, for "sin constantly becomes, not by necessity but by freedom."[22]

This interpretation of sin is guided by the Letter of James as well as by Aristotelian metaphysics, and provides a fascinating illustration of the way Kierkegaard combines philosophical and biblical influences. When Vigilus Haufniensis attempts to understand the narrative of the Fall, he turns to James for illumination. The Letter of James begins with the theme of temptation, teaching that those who endure temptation are blessed:

> Let no man say when he is tempted, I am tempted by God: for God cannot be tempted with evil, and tempts no-one. But every man is tempted, when he is drawn away by his own desire. Desire, when it is conceived, brings forth sin: and sin, when it is finished, brings forth death.

Does this mean that the serpent in the story is mythical, a symbol of desire? Were Adam and Eve tempted by their own desire? How, then, did this desire awaken? Turning back to the Genesis narrative, we can identify God's command not to eat from the tree of knowledge as a pivotal moment—for this command creates a possibility; creates, indeed, possibility itself. For the first time, God's words do not completely correspond to what is, to actuality, to His will; language is no longer fully affirmative. With the prohibition language deviates from being, gains a life of its own, and provides the chance for reflection. The serpent asks Eve what God said: "*did* he say that you should not . . . ?", awakening a possibility, a desire, a sense of something lacking, a feeling of anxiety. Does the serpent, then, represent language (a tongue) as well as desire? And is it this that creates interiority itself? In any case, one might say that God's command awakens the potentiality of sin within the individual, but that it is the individual who actualizes this possibility and becomes sinful. In *The Concept of Anxiety* we find once more a critique of Hegel that focuses on the issue of movement, emphasizing the immanence and impotence of mediation:

> Mediation is equivocal . . . it designates movement but at the same time rest . . . In logic no movement can *come about*, for logic *is*, and everything logical simply is, and this impotence of logic is the transition to the sphere of becoming where existence and reality appear . . . in logic every movement (if for an instant one would use this expression) is an immanent movement, which in a deeper sense is no movement, as one will easily convince oneself if one reflects that the very concept of movement is a transcendence which can find no place in logic.[23]

The pseudonym Vigilus Haufniensis adds in a note to this passage that "the eternal expression of logic is that which the Eleatic School transferred by mistake to existence: Nothing comes into existence; everything is."

In the *Sickness Unto Death* a new pseudonym, Anti-Climacus, returns to the question of sin and offers an analysis that emphasizes inward movements of intensification and elevation. Sin, like faith and repentance, seems to be a form of repetition:

> 'the continuance of sin' . . . does not mean the particular new sins as much as the state of sin, which in turn becomes the internal intensification of sin, a conscious remaining in the state of sin, so that the law of motion in intensification, here as elsewhere, is inward, in greater and greater intensity of consciousness.[24]

This horribly obscure passage manages to say something very direct about how inwardness and movement are essential to one another, how each cannot be without the other, and how together they form the soul.

Chapter Eight

∞

Beyond Philosophy?

One of the most important accomplishments of our focus on the theme of movement is to give some insight into Kierkegaard's relationship to the philosophical tradition, and to illuminate the ambivalence of this relationship. We have seen that the question of motion constitutes, on the one hand, Kierkegaard's point of contact with the philosophical tradition: in enquiring about the transition from non-being to being he shares with both ancient and modern thinkers a starting point for the pursuit of truth. Also, it is through the question of motion, as mediation, that Kierkegaard engages with the intellectual debates of his contemporaries in Copenhagen. On the other hand, however, movement incites a questioning of the value of philosophical reflection, because it signifies for Kierkegaard the *actuality* of existence, the *power* of becoming, which cannot be appropriated by thought. The revaluation implicit in Kierkegaard's thematization of movement rejects Hegelian philosophy, criticizes academia, and offers "a polemic against the truth as knowledge." In place of these established forms of thought, Kierkegaard presents a kind of reconstruction of the Christian consciousness, suggesting in the first place that the power for actualization lies in—indeed, is synonymous with—the existing individual's inwardness or soul (freedom), and in the second place that the origin of this power is God (transcendence). This revaluation and reconstruction suggests a movement from idea to existence, from philosophy to faith.

We have seen that the 1843 texts cannot be properly understood without recognizing how they are directed toward the tasks and the teachings of Christianity. However, this need not lead us to conclude that Kierkegaard should not be considered as a philosopher, or that we should exclude him from discourse that remains purely philosophical. On the contrary, Kierkegaard's interest in movement demonstrates his profound engagement with what Heidegger calls "the question of being"—with the ontological question that lies within every genuine philosophy. By focusing on the issue of motion, Kierkegaard penetrates straight to the heart of philosophical thinking: he reaches back into the western tradition, takes hold of the concept of kinesis, and reshapes it in the existential sphere, arguing that *becoming* is an actualizing movement, an expression of power, and that *becoming a Christian* requires openness to God as the source of all power.[1]

Even though he rejects Greek categories such as recollection because they cannot adequately articulate the task of Christianity, Kierkegaard still thinks with the Greeks insofar as he poses again the profound, simple, and unnerving question of becoming. Questions about motion arise from an encounter with the *difference* between non-being and being: how does something come into being? What, or who, accomplishes this transition? The question of movement is an ontological question and a starting point of philosophy: it tries to identify the power of existence, the 'in-itself' of things.

Constructing an ontology means articulating the way in which things are related to the power that grounds them. Aristotle's ontology, for example, envisages a cosmos of beings emulating an eternal, divine final cause, so that finite existence can be understood and evaluated in terms of desiring and responding to an unchanging good. We have already considered how the 'plane of motion' suggested by Kierkegaard's writing differs from that of ancient Greek philosophy: for Kierkegaard the transition from non-being to being takes place not in the cosmos but in the soul, the interiority of the existing individual. A plane of motion is the locus of truth, and Kierkegaard's plane of motion can be identified as the individual's consciousness or subjectivity. Posing the question of becoming in this sphere, Kierkegaard's concern is the same as Aristotle's: to explore how existing beings relate to their grounding power. In each of the 1843 texts, the theme of movement leads the reader through the ontological enquiry that constitutes philosophy and toward the specific teachings of Christianity—toward a transcendent, loving God who gives all existence as a gift. The question of how the individual is related to this original power is posed existentially as the task of becoming a Christian.

Kierkegaard includes philosophy within the aesthetic sphere, and as we have seen aesthetic literature can be edifying insofar as it accomplishes some movement toward a Christian life. If philosophy can be edifying, it can be religious—and of course we need not rely on Kierkegaard to demonstrate this. For Augustine, for example, God is the focus of his enquiry into truth and the light that illuminates his soul, allowing him to reason and to understand. In his *Confessions* Augustine addresses his philosophical questions to God and thanks Him for the insights he gains. For Augustine as for Kierkegaard, God is truth and love, and the source of all things. "God is present as a whole everywhere—*just like Truth*, which no one in their right mind would say is partly in this place and partly in that; *for after all Truth is God.*" This conviction guides Augustine's inward inquiry "into the new dimension of the soul, the inner space that is not literally a space."[2] Most medieval philosophy is also deeply religious, to the extent that metaphysical speculation can be an expression of faith and a form of worship. Even Spinoza's philosophy, which positions itself outside institutional and doctrinal religion, inquires into God as the grounding power of finite things, and as truth itself. This ontological thinking is thoroughly religious, for it seeks to uncover the blessedness and love of God and suggests a way of living in accordance with this truth. We might even describe Heidegger's philosophy as religious, for even though it refuses to address God it strives for an inward opening to Being beyond ourselves—and here Heidegger echoes Kierkegaard and seems to owe much to him.

∞

If it is too much to claim that Kierkegaard's writing moves beyond philosophy, can we say instead that it moves beyond Hegelian thought? The emphasis on movement in the pseudonymous texts makes it clear that they are in continual dialogue with Hegel, and in particular with the principle of mediation. Kierkegaard's claim that the dialectical method does not allow for 'real' movement articulates a critique of Hegel from the perspective of the task of becoming a Christian. Against Hegel, he insists that truth is subjective and its movements inward: distinct from the external, social world and beyond the powers of reason. While Hegelian philosophers aspire to pure thought, Kierkegaard values purity of heart. As Johannes Climacus says in the *Postscript*,

> The philosopher contemplates Christianity for the sake of interpenetrating it with his speculative thought . . . But suppose that this whole proceeding were a chimera, a sheer impossibility; suppose that Christianity is subjectivity, an inner transformation, an actualization of inwardness, and *that only two kinds of people can know anything about it*: those who with an *infinite passionate interest* in an eternal happiness base this their happiness upon their believing relationship to Christianity,

and those who with an opposite passion, but *in passion*, reject it—*the happy and unhappy lovers*.[3]

Kierkegaard argues that Hegel's philosophy, like academic life, is existentially impotent because it remains disinterested. An individual's power—his ability to make movements, to become religious—corresponds to his passion. In 1841 Kierkegaard remarked in his journal that "passion is the real thing, the real measure of man's power. And the age in which we live is wretched, because it is without passion."

Kierkegaard is concerned with movements of reaching beyond, or transcending—for example, the movement beyond reflection into existence. He equates the immanence of Hegelian thought with its impotence. In the movement of the dialectic, according to the principle of mediation, consciousness or 'spirit' makes explicit what is already implicit, and the distinction between internal and external is overcome in the dynamic reciprocity of self-explication and self-recognition. Kierkegaard objects that nothing new can emerge from this process and that it allows no room for freedom: Hegel has tried "to make movement fundamental in a sphere where movement is unthinkable."[4]

For Kierkegaard, Hegelian philosophy is incompatible with Christianity because the latter occupies a plane of motion, or a form of temporality, that is distinct from world history. Filled with God's power, inwardness has infinite passion and intensity, and this intensity can be expressed in temporal terms as the eternal (an assimilation that does not apply only to religious passion: intense romantic love includes the conviction that it is 'forever'). The Christian's relationship to God transforms his existence by raising it to the significance of eternity, of an eternal happiness. For Hegel, though, subjectivity cannot be separated from objectivity, from history, from the world. Viewed from an external perspective, Christianity *is* historical—as, indeed, are Christians themselves—but within a Christian life time itself changes: the individual's relationship to God is at once eternal and "contemporaneous." This is not to deny that the Incarnation revealing life's eternity was an historical fact; Kierkegaard least of all would do so, for precisely this constitutes the paradox of Christ.

The polemic against the objectivity and immanence of the Hegelian system seems to imply that the speculative philosopher attempts to usurp the position of God. Kierkegaard does not go so far as accusing Hegelians of sin and heresy, but he does suggest that their philosophy is a work of supreme arrogance:

> Reality itself is a system—for God; but it cannot be a system for any existing spirit … But who is the systematic thinker? It is he who is outside of existence, who is in his eternity forever complete, and yet includes all existence within himself—it is God … The point of view of immanence exists only for contemplation, essentially and in truth only for God, and as an illusion for worshipful professors.[5]

As we have seen, Kierkegaard tends to conflate Hegel's philosophy, his Hegelian contemporaries in Denmark, and academia in general. His writing certainly tries to move beyond this interpretation of Hegel, which is confined to the aesthetic sphere. But what about the 'real' Hegel? How far does his philosophy resemble Kierkegaard's caricature of "the System," and how vulnerable is it to the critique articulated through the theme of movement? If we begin to study Hegel after reading Kierkegaard, we may find ourselves surprised by the depth of his analysis of religious faith, by his emphasis on love, and by the spiritual quality of his philosophy as a whole. There certainly seems to be truth in Hegel's insight that subjectivity and objectivity are substantially the same, and continually reflecting, forming and manifesting one another. Anyone with pantheistic sympathies will find nothing deficient in the immanence of his philosophy: why do we need a supernatural divine Creator if both nature and spirit are forces or 'moments' of the absolute itself?

Kierkegaard and Hegel appear to be irreconcilable. Although they both insist on movement, they assume different positions and occupy different planes. Does this mean that we have to choose between them—to decide that one thinker is right and the other wrong? Or would it be possible to argue that in some way they are both right? As it happens, Kierkegaard's view that philosophy belongs to the aesthetic sphere can help to shed some light on this. Reflection is aesthetic insofar as it is "disinterested" in reality or existence; whether or not something exists makes no difference to the engagement of the aesthete or thinker, for he is confined to the realm of possibility. "From the poetic and intellectual standpoint, possibility is higher than reality, the aesthetic and intellectual being disinterested. There is only one interest, the interest in existence; disinterestedness is therefore the expression for indifference to reality."[6] This echoes the account of aesthetic experience presented by Kant in his *Critique of Judgment*—and it is interesting that Kant's theory of taste can be applied to our judgments about philosophies as well as about aesthetic objects. Indeed, Kierkegaard makes precisely this connection in a note to *The Concept of Anxiety*, where he suggests that "metaphysics is disinterested, as Kant affirms of aesthetics."

Very briefly, Kant's account of judgments of taste—claims such as "this rose is beautiful"—appeals to four criteria: universality, necessity, disinterestedness, and purposiveness. These judgments are based on subjective experience, but they involve an implicit expectation that others will agree so long as they approach the object in the same way and under the same conditions. Because one is indifferent to the reality of the object one cannot desire it; because the object as schematized by the imagination exhibits a purely formal purposiveness, the understanding can "play" with it freely without determining its content under a specific concept. This harmonious "free play" of the faculties gives rise to a feeling of pleasure that does not require sensory gratification, and which expresses itself in the statement "this is beautiful." During an aesthetic experience, the individual is free from questions of existence and determination: she is in the sphere of possibility.

The delight felt by a reader or a student who begins to appreciate a particular work of philosophy resembles the aesthetic pleasure described by Kant. Is the judgment that a philosophy is 'right' or 'true' based on its correspondence to reality, or on the pleasure of reflecting on the harmonious interrelation of parts and whole? Is it incoherent to find truth in two philosophies that make different metaphysical claims, or to admire a philosophy that conflicts with one's own opinions? It is often not a specific position that appeals to us—for example, Christianity or atheism, idealism, or materialism—but the coherence and the style of the whole view. People who like Kierkegaard tend to like Nietzsche too. When we read, write, and argue about a work of philosophy, we recreate or imagine it (in the Kantian sense), and communicate this work to others by means of concepts, metaphors, reasoning, and propositions, so that they too can behold it and turn it this way and that to admire it. Just as aesthetic experience is mediated by the sensible appearance of its object, yet the judgment of taste is based on formal qualities that facilitate that playful activity of the mind, so one's encounter with a philosophy is mediated by concepts and so on, yet is fulfilled only when the understanding runs freely through the whole. (Deleuze's cryptic suggestion that "the problem of thought is the problem of infinite speed" seems to indicate something like this.)

Kierkegaard's thought exhibits coherence and integrity, as our focus on the themes of inwardness and becoming accentuates; Hegelian philosophy certainly makes explicit the interrelations of parts and whole. And they both express important truths about becoming. In a way, each contains the other's thought within itself: inwardness is a moment of the dialectic of spirit, and 'Hegel' is the position that seeks to move beyond itself, out of the aesthetic sphere. From an historical perspective, too, it is easy to see how Kierkegaard's writing is formed by and responsive to his social, intellectual, and spiritual milieu. Perhaps we can only move back and forth between Hegel and Kierkegaard, attending to them alternately and on their own terms, rather as we look at paintings and listen to pieces of music one at a time.

Kierkegaard's assimilation of the intellectual and the aesthetic need not imply, for us, a negative or limited estimation of philosophy. The aesthetic sphere has its own mode of valuation; works of art have their own kinds of truth, for they can move us, inspire us, and reveal something to us. Indeed, Nietzsche argues that aesthetic criteria are the only ones we have for discriminating between things, making them meaningful, and calling them good or bad—and many writers, especially during the last few decades, happily emphasize the continuities between philosophical texts and works of art. Wittgenstein once remarked that, far from viewing metaphysics as worthless, he regarded "some of the great philosophical systems of the past as among the noblest productions of the human mind," which suggests that we can still read and appreciate metaphysics as works of art.[7] Deleuze suggests that philosophy consists in creating concepts, and his own writing is intensely aesthetic. Perhaps we learn more from philosophy when we ask not what it proves but what it expresses and how it affects us—for this reason, it is a shame that many recent thinkers are so preoccupied by the "death" or the "end" of metaphysics. And perhaps our philosophies, including religious philosophies and even sacred teachings themselves, are like intellectual tapestries, inward and unfinished, with which we adorn our worlds to make them beautiful and bright.[8]

∞

I have suggested that Kierkegaard's authorship as a whole is directed toward the task of becoming a Christian, and that the theme of movement helps to reveal this orientation in places where it is not explicit. It is clear that Kierkegaard's writing cannot be fully understood without appreciating its religious position. However, this need not prevent us from considering whether the interpretation of becoming that we have brought to light has philosophical value outside a Christian context.

One philosopher of the European tradition who may help us here is Spinoza, whose *Ethics* offers a full account of the nature of God, of human beings, and of the relationship between them, without commitment to a particular religious doctrine. Spinoza argues that God is a unique, infinite, eternal substance, and can be identified with nature: everything that is, is in God, and God is the immanent rather than the transitive cause of all things. The free will of individuals, and their separateness from the whole, is an illusion. The highest good is intellectual knowledge of God. At first sight this philosophy of immanence—which, after all, inspired Hegel—seems very far removed from Kierkegaard's insistence that God is transcendent, absolutely different, and unknowable. However, the ontological interpretation that has eventually emerged from our focus on the theme of movement, and which captures the essence of Kierkegaard's thought—*the self as a center of power, and God as the source of all power*—is integral to Spinoza's *Ethics* too.

Kierkegaard is not the sort of thinker who offers a definition of the human being, but implicit in his writing is an interpretation of individuality in terms of inward movement. Johannes de silentio does venture to say that "the essentially human is passion," and as we have seen passion is a movement of intensification that can be equated with inwardness itself. From a 'directly' religious perspective, Kierkegaard can more straightforwardly identify the soul as the essence of the existing individual—and this soul is a movement, for it "inclosingly spins." The power or capacity of the soul depends on the extent to which it opens itself to God's power, and this degree of power corresponds to the intensity of its movement.

Spinoza also interprets individuality in terms of movement. More specifically, an individual endures, or maintains its identity, for as long as it preserves a certain "ratio of motion and rest." This preservation is itself something active, expressive of power, for each individual "endeavors to persist in being," or strives to repeat itself. Finite beings, or modes, are distinguished from each other not by means of substance—for there are no substances other than God—but by their proportion of motion and rest, or "speed or slowness." "The essence of the mode is a degree of power, a part of the divine power, i.e. an intensive part or a degree of intensity."[9] Spinoza's view that substance, the self-causing power of existence, is singular and infinite also means that God and the individual cannot be distinguished by means of substance: man is in God, and God is within each man. All power is God's power—and this has to be the case since power *is* that which causes itself, or "is in itself," which in turn is the definition of substance. So for Spinoza as for Kierkegaard the self is a center of power, and God is the source of all power. God is the origin that repeats itself, and in so doing expresses itself; God is a movement, a power, rather than a thing. To become religious is to understand that this power which spontaneously pours forth is a *loving* power: that this is the same love—the same because it continually becomes new—as that which flows through beings and between them.

This does not mean that we should make light of the differences between Spinoza and Kierkegaard. Their doctrinal beliefs, their estimations of the value of philosophical thinking, and their temperaments are certainly very far apart. But ontologically, or metaphysically—though neither position sits easily with the idea of metaphysics—they seem to have something in common. This raises questions about Kierkegaard's insistence on transcendence. As I have suggested, for Kierkegaard this signifies divine power, and also a movement of reaching beyond—beyond reflection, beyond the finite world, beyond self-assertion, beyond resignation. Although he seems unconcerned with the objective truth about God, Kierkegaard's emphasis on transcendence distinguishes him from a nonrealist interpretation of religious faith, since a transcendent God *has to have power*, has to be the source of actuality. But does this God, who is at work in the inwardness of every being (which can include nature as a whole), need to be separate from finite things? If Kierkegaard sees the self as a center of power, and God as the source of all power, can the human and the divine be conceived as substantially distinct? And is this kind of distinction required by the view that the Christian incarnation is a paradox? So long as the difference between eternity and finitude is irreducible—as indeed it is for Spinoza—their intersection in the life of Christ remains paradoxical. The *Ethics* shows that God and finite beings can be ontologically distinct—and the latter absolutely dependent on the former—without being different substances.

Kierkegaard does not raise these metaphysical questions, and he would have no reason to deviate from his quite conservative theological position. However, from a Kierkegaardian perspective, whether God created the world as described in the Book of Genesis, or is the cause of all things in some other way, is a secondary issue that does not necessarily affect the requirements of religious faith. This allows us to explore Kierkegaard's interpretation of human existence, and its relationship to God, beyond a dogmatic Christian context, so that it might illuminate spiritual "tasks of becoming" which belong to different positions.

Chapter Nine

Repetitions

If the theme of movement connects Kierkegaard to the philosophical tradition that precedes him, in particular to Greek metaphysics and to Hegelian thought, it also illuminates the significance of his writing in relation to more recent thinkers. Indeed, one could argue that modern existentialism began in 1843 with the proclamation of repetition as the new category of truth, expressive of an actualizing movement as opposed to an idealizing movement. Focusing on the theme of movement should help us to read Kierkegaard in the context of a philosophical discourse concerning selfhood, power, and becoming that more usually looks to Nietzsche and Heidegger for guidance.

The question of movement provides an enlightening starting point for comparing the writings of Kierkegaard and Nietzsche. Nietzsche, like Kierkegaard, employs an evaluative vocabulary of power, strength, and vitality in opposition to the traditional philosophical interpretation of the truth as knowledge: he finds himself concerned with "nothing but questions of strength: how far to oppose truth and to reflect on its most questionable sides?"[1] Nietzsche, like Kierkegaard, nevertheless excavates Greek philosophy, takes a doctrine of movement—in his case, eternal recurrence—and applies it to the existing individual as a kind of ethical test.[2] Nietzsche, like Kierkegaard, regards the existing individual as a center of power: "I require the starting point of 'will to power' as the origin of motion. Hence motion may not be conditioned from the outside—not caused—I require beginnings and centers of motion from which the will spreads."[3] Of course, Nietzsche's proclamation of the death of God not only disconnects the self from any kind of transcendent ground, but also disregards the protective seal that Kierkegaard builds (or upbuilds) around inwardness. He rejects the notions of a 'thing in itself' and an inward subject, and instead offers a monist, expressivist vision of becoming: "there is no 'being' behind doing, effecting, becoming; 'the doer' is merely a fiction added to the deed—the deed is everything."[4] However, we may question whether this critique of essence undermines Kierkegaard's particular interpretation of inwardness, which is not a being behind becoming or a subject underlying activity, but rather a movement of opening *to* becoming. More likely to divide the philosophers are their evaluative characterizations of two basic existential (op)positions: receptive versus self-centered (Kierkegaard), and active versus reactive (Nietzsche). These two orders of rank recognize not just degrees but qualities of power. Do their highest values, receptivity and activity—and their lower values, selfishness and reactivity—contradict or correspond to one another?

One of the most important differences between Kierkegaard and Nietzsche lies in their estimation of the aesthetic approach to life. Nietzsche melts down the vertical axis of Kierkegaard's spiritual movement and, in opposition to the supernatural repetition claimed by Christianity, proposes incessant renewal as the essence of nature itself. For Nietzsche, it is only on the basis of aesthetic criteria that individuals can infuse the indiscriminate power of nature with any kind of value. In relation to Nietzsche it no longer makes sense to speak of an aesthetic 'sphere' distinct from other modes of valuation: the power of beings (and the "good health" of the culture to which they belong) is measured by their creativity—by their ability to *create values*. This contrasts starkly with Kierkegaard's denigration of the aesthetic as impotent and as inferior to the ethical and the religious, and also with his dismissal of repetition in the natural world. Despite these differences, however, both Kierkegaard and Nietzsche look to movement as a way of overcoming the nihilism that results from the Platonic-Hegelian tradition of philosophy. Movement is integral to the existential task confronting the individual in a nihilistic age, whether this task takes the form of becoming a Christian or of creating values.[5]

In *Difference and Repetition* Deleuze presents a comparison between Kierkegaard and Nietzsche that addresses these issues. Regarding Nietzsche's account of the eternal recurrence as a form of repetition, he suggests that for both thinkers this is the movement that is to carry philosophy forward: "There is a force common to Kierkegaard and Nietzsche . . . Each, in his own way, makes repetition the fundamental category of a philosophy of the future."[6] Deleuze goes on to analyze the points upon which their movements converge: repetition is a way of liberation;

it opposes the laws of nature and morality; and it also opposes the forces of habit and memory through which the past determines the process of becoming—a project developed by Freud, whose own concept of repetition expresses precisely this constraining power of the past. Both Kierkegaard and Nietzsche incorporate the movement of repetition into their literary style: they "bring to philosophy new means of expression" and they want "to put metaphysics in motion, in action."[7] On the basis of this comparison, Deleuze suggests, the essential divergence between the two thinkers can be understood more clearly:

> It then becomes easy to speak of the differences between Kierkegaard and Nietzsche. Even this question, however, must no longer be posed at the speculative level of the ultimate nature of the God of Abraham or the Dionysus of Zarathustra. It is rather a matter of knowing what it means to "produce movement," to repeat or to obtain repetition. Is it a matter of leaping, as Kierkegaard believes? Or is it rather a matter of dancing, as Nietzsche thinks? . . . Nietzsche's leading idea is to ground the repetition in eternal return on the death of God and the dissolution of the self. Kierkegaard dreams of an alliance between a God and a self rediscovered. All sorts of differences follow: is the movement in the sphere of the mind, or in the entrails of the earth which knows neither God nor self? Where will it be better protected against generalities, against mediations?[8]

These questions remain unanswered, but they illuminate the choice presented by Kierkegaard's and Nietzsche's accounts of movement—and, more generally, between Christianity and atheism. In the Conclusion to *Difference and Repetition* Deleuze suggests that each vision of repetition presents its own articulation of the basic structure of temporality: "in the case of Kierkegaard it is repetition itself which takes place once and for all, whereas according to Nietzsche it operates for all times."[9]

∞

Thinkers who have been inspired by Kierkegaard and Nietzsche may be approached within the new philosophical horizon opened up between their two forms of repetition. One of the questions brought to light through this opening is that of the origin of becoming: can this movement be traced back to a transcendent source, infused with the value that is bestowed by God's love? Or is it empty of value and meaning until appropriated by a creative individual? In the wake of Kierkegaard and Nietzsche, the question of the origin of existence asks also, *where does meaning come from?* Addressing this question it is Heidegger, above all other philosophers, who steps into the 'between' set out by Kierkegaard and Nietzsche.

In Heidegger's *Being and Time* the question of movement takes the form of an enquiry into temporality, from the perspective of human existence (*Dasein*, or 'being-there'). This means that time is interpreted in terms of 'lifetime': the time of our lives, the stretches of time that we each ourselves are; the time that concerns us and makes us anxious, because we have to decide how to spend it without having knowledge or control of its end toward which we inexorably move. "The movement of existence is not the motion of something present-at-hand. It is definable in terms of the way Dasein stretches along."[10] Heidegger calls this movement the "historizing" or the "historicality" of *Dasein*, and states that existential authenticity (his first formulation for truth) is achieved through repetition: "when historicality is authentic, it understands history as the 'recurrence' of the possible, and knows that a possibility will recur only if existence is open for it fatefully, in a moment of vision, in resolute repetition."[11]

So whose repetition is this—Kierkegaard's or Nietzsche's? Heidegger's existential categories in *Being and Time* certainly seem to owe much to Kierkegaard, but on the other hand his philosophical inquiry tries to exclude the Christian perspective within which Kierkegaardian repetition has its meaning. The God who, for Kierkegaard, is the source of all repetition and thus the beginning and the end of any Christian's ontological questioning, is bracketed by Heidegger as a merely "ontic" concern.[12] The Being addressed by Heidegger's initial project of ontology seems closer to Nietzschean recurrence than to Kierkegaardian repetition. In any case, he follows both thinkers in recognizing the aporia of movement as essential to the question of Being: he concludes his analysis of Dasein's historicality with the remark that "everything is haunted by the *enigma* of Being, and, as has now been made plain, by that of *motion*."[13] This suggestion of a close connection between Being and movement indicates that Kierkegaard's writings, though largely unacknowledged by Heidegger, provide an indispensable background to *Being and Time* if only insofar as they raise the question of motion from the perspective of situated, individual existence, or Dasein.

Heidegger's suggestion, inspired by Husserl, that the being of Dasein is always and essentially 'being-in-the-world' challenges the dualistic separation of subject and object exemplified by Cartesian philosophy. Does this also raise an objection to Kierkegaard's insistence, against Hegel, on the difference—and, indeed, the incommensurability—between the internal and the external? And where would this leave inwardness? In Kierkegaard's defense, we might argue that his interpretation of consciousness is already phenomenological (though not, of course, explicitly and methodologically so like Heidegger's), and that the degrees of inwardness represented by the aesthetic, ethical, and religious spheres involve particular ways of relating to the world. On the other hand, though, Heidegger's emphasis on the contextual and relational character of existence can provide an important corrective to interpretations of Kierkegaard that are too individualistic and isolationist. Personal relationships are the principle, the basic category, of Kierkegaard's thought: he replaces the dialectical movement between concepts with the reciprocal movements of love and loss, of giving and receiving, between individuals. It is in this sense that Kierkegaard's philosophy is thoroughly theological; Heidegger sees this as a weakness, while Kierkegaard regards it as an expression of the highest spiritual strength.

As Heidegger's thinking develops after *Being and Time*, movement remains integral to his interpretation of truth. His insistence that truth must be understood in terms of the Greek *aletheia*—which means "unconcealment," bringing something out of darkness or oblivion—opposes the notions of representation and correspondence that characterize the accounts of truth offered by traditional philosophy. For Heidegger, representation and correspondence are possible only on the basis of a more original movement of "clearing," *lichtung*, the letting-appear of beings as such. He suggests, moreover, that this movement signifies freedom: "To lighten something means to make it light, free and open, e.g., to make the forest free of trees at one place. The free space thus originating is the clearing."[14] Heidegger's etymological discussion of the term "clearing" emphasizes its dynamism and activity: he penetrates the static appearance of the noun *lichtung* by tracing it back to the verb *lichten*. This transition from noun to verb, from thing to process, is an important force within Heidegger's thought, essential for grasping his philosophical interpretation of Being.

Truth as aletheia is "a becoming and happening."[15] The simultaneous revelation and concealment ("the double movement of clearing and veiling")[16] that is integral to this form of truth echoes Kierkegaard's discussion of love in the 1843 discourses on *Love Will Hide a Multitude of Sins*. Here, love is a form of truth that discovers the good as it hides sinfulness or impurity—and perhaps it is this to which Heidegger refers in his comment that "there is more to be learnt philosophically from [Kierkegaard's] 'edifying' writings than from his theoretical ones."[17] The similarity between these two movements of truth raises some interesting questions about the way in which truth "happens." For Kierkegaard, the event of truth occurs only in the individual's inwardness, for this is where God's love is given and received. Heidegger, on the other hand, is also interested in the way in which truth is disclosed in more tangible structures, especially works of art.

In his essay "The End of Philosophy and the Task of Thinking" —which was originally written for a conference on Kierkegaard—Heidegger proposes "Thinking" as an alternative to the traditional philosophical pursuit of truth. This Thinking begins with a confrontation with the unknown, and thus proceeds by *questioning*. We can view this in the context of Kierkegaard's project if we recognize that his account of existential truth as facing the future must inevitably be oriented toward something unknown. From Kierkegaard's Christian perspective the future is possessed by God and becomes present through His continual bestowal of existence as a gift. For both Heidegger and Kierkegaard, the unknown is essential to truth, and for this reason knowledge is an inadequate method for the pursuit of truth. Although Heidegger's version of the unknown belongs to a truth event supposedly more primordial than any notion of God, his Thinking *as questioning* retains the qualities of expectancy and patience advocated by Kierkegaard in the first and last of his 1843 discourses. This rather mystical Thinking "is content with awakening a readiness in man for a possibility whose contour remains obscure, whose coming remains uncertain."[18]

"The End of Philosophy and the Task of Thinking" exemplifies the shift in Heidegger's later thinking toward recognition of something "beyond" man—a departure from the more Nietzschean horizon of *Being and Time*. He comes more and more to interpret Being as something that is given—as a gift—which reconnects to Kierkegaard's concern with the transcendent source of existence. For Heidegger, however, this source is not God, apprehended through faith, but an insoluble aporia, apprehended through another question: he concludes the essay by asking, "But where does the clearing come from and how is it given? What speaks in the 'There is/It gives'?"[19] Although the existential power that Kierkegaard traces back to God remains an enigma for Heidegger, he nevertheless advocates a relationship to becoming that resembles the receptive activity of faith. He describes Thinking as thanking, as letting-be, as openness to the event of truth. These qualities are emphasized in one of Heidegger's last pieces of writing, the dialogue "on a country path" published in his *Discourse on Thinking*. Here Heidegger reflects on the idea of "releasement" (*Gelassenheit*), and proposes Heraclitus's fragment *agkibasia*, or "going toward," as a description of thinking, of finding the truth. In addition to the dynamic symbolism of the thinkers' journey through the woodland, we find the suggestion that "waiting moves into openness . . . releasement [is] not only a path but a movement."[20] The dialogue's final formulation for releasement is "moving-into-nearness."

∽

Existentialist philosophy begins with Kierkegaard's account of Christian faith—but what happens to existentialism when God (the source of all power) is taken away? What happens to the self as a center of power when it is cut off from its divine origin? We have seen how Nietzsche affirms precisely this: proclaiming that the earth is now "unchained from its sun," he happily throws aside the question of grounds.[21] This leaves only the self as the center of power, but this activity of willing can hardly be called a self any more. Nietzsche prefers to think more in terms of a *life* than of a self, and here "life" signifies a natural movement. Expressivism and naturalism are two of the most important aspects of Nietzsche's philosophy, and they indicate its dynamism.

We have also seen how Heidegger, though following Nietzsche in offering a 'death of God' philosophy, drifts some way back toward Kierkegaard's existentialist vision. The guiding lights of self and God that Nietzsche extinguished are rekindled a little by Heidegger: although he rejects the solidified 'subject' of traditional philosophy, *Being and Time* emphasizes the individuality of Dasein—the "mineness" of its death and thus of the temporality that this death gives meaning to. This text presents a mode of existential truth (authenticity) which, with its orientation toward the future and its decisiveness, is explicitly reminiscent of Kierkegaard's category of repetition.

For Kierkegaard the question of movement or power is linked intimately with the question of *the ground of existence*, and this question emerges once again for Heidegger, from the ontological project of *Being and Time* to his later, more poetic thinking. Heidegger's invocation of the ground of being, in one sense a turning away from Nietzsche, is nevertheless steeped in Nietzsche's naturalism—this ground is earthy, real: the earth itself jutting forth into the world; the forest clearing; questions as pathways through dusky woodlands. One gets a sense that, situated in this place between Kierkegaard and Nietzsche, Heidegger is a thinker on rather uncertain ground, where he is vulnerable to accusations of profound inauthenticity, whether as a philosopher or as an existing individual. In the wake of the death of God, at a dark moment in history, the ground is precarious, and so we find a rather tentative mood pervading Heidegger's later writing.

John-Paul Sartre offers a third version of atheist existentialism, and his is structurally the most faithful to Kierkegaard's philosophical position. Unlike Heidegger, Sartre engages explicitly and positively with Kierkegaard's writing—I would also add, less kindly, that his philosophy lacks any significant originality. Sartre can be read as describing what happens to a Kierkegaardian individual who is disconnected from God: the absence of grounds for his existence ("nothingness") is a brute fact that reveals that life is absurd, in either a comic or a tragic sense. In his interpretation of the self as an *ungrounded* center of power, Sartre emphasizes its radical freedom, its contingency. In addition to his philosophical works, Sartre dramatizes this view of the human situation in novels such as *Nausea* and the *Roads to Freedom* trilogy.

In *Nausea* Sartre presents a very interesting variation on the themes of movement and ground. In the famous scene in the park at six o'clock, Roquentin stares at the root of a tree and becomes overwhelmed by the density, the unremitting protrusion of existence itself. This is an encounter with repetition: with a Nietzschean, natural repetition apprehended without faith or courage. Again individuality is articulated through a vocabulary of power, but Sartre emphasizes "weaknesses, frailties." Roquentin sees "beings without origin," without reason, without meaning, but he cannot summon the optimism and affirmation of Nietzsche's heroes:

> So many existences failed and stubbornly begun again and once more failed—like the clumsy efforts of an insect which had fallen on its back? (I was one of those efforts). That abundance did not give the impression of generosity, far from it . . . There were fools who talked to you about willpower and the struggle for life . . . Impossible to see things that way. Weaknesses, frailties, yes. The trees were floating. Thrusting towards the sky? Collapsing rather . . . They did not want to exist, only they could not help it, that was the point . . . they were too weak to die, because death could come to them only from the outside . . . Every existence is born without reason, prolongs itself out of weakness and dies by chance.[22]

There is an air of impotence surrounding Sartre's characters: a sense of futility and of boundless indifference, of acute boredom verging on laughter—the kind of nihilism summed up in the image of a chain-smoking philosopher. Although these types are more stylish than Kierkegaard's aesthetic characters (they are French, after all), they likewise fall short of a paradigm of existential power such as Abraham: they are depressed, alienated, and antisocial, unable to transform their sufferings through loving relationships; unable to enjoy their lives. This once more presents a correspondence between strength and happiness, impotence and *ennui*, which helps to illuminate the existentialist preoccupation with power and movement.

∞

What can we, now, learn from Kierkegaard? As we have seen, his thematization of movement proposes "a polemic against the truth as knowledge" and a new mode of valuation according to love. Although his critics may equate this with irrationalism, I suggest that, on the contrary, the theme of movement indicates not only the coherence of Kierkegaard's writing but also its philosophical integrity: categories such as inwardness and faith are rooted in Aristotle's concept of kinesis, and they invoke a plane of motion that has its own form of truth. One of Kierkegaard's great achievements is to establish a philosophical perspective from which to approach the teaching that *love* constitutes the essence of Christianity—and, of course, this insight into the meaning and significance of love is relevant to other religions too, as well as to human life in general. So, despite Kierkegaard's undeniable anti-intellectualism, he nevertheless offers concepts, and even a kind of logic, that bring clarity to an aspect of existence which, perhaps more than any other, presents a challenge to our understanding.[23]

Kierkegaard's view that the pursuit of knowledge may tempt us away from the truth, and in any case is unsuitable as a method for approaching religious questions, may be extreme—but it is nevertheless compelling, and should at least be considered carefully. For this reason, the philosophical tradition known as existentialism, which can to some extent be defined by the opposition to the truth as knowledge exemplified by Kierkegaard's writing, remains a vital source of inspiration for philosophers of religion. Modern existentialist thought seems particularly relevant in the present time, when communities (such as cities, schools, and families)—and sometimes individuals themselves—accommodate diverse religious traditions. The shift to asking 'how?' rather than 'what?' opens up interpretations of the human situation, of the individual's being-in-the-world, that can help us to approach questions shared by different doctrines and forms of faith. For example, thinkers such as Kierkegaard and Nietzsche teach us to understand freedom not as an abstract idea, but as a task of liberation and empowerment.

Kierkegaard's account of movement illuminates the significance of existentialism. Becoming is the essence or the truth of existence—and we can trace this insight back to the ancient Greek questions of motion. Movement expresses power: the power of coming-into-being, of actualization. Existentialist philosophy explores this theme of power from the perspective of subjectivity; it could even be defined as *a thinking concerned with movement in the sphere of the existing individual*. Sartre's statement that "existence precedes essence" makes explicit the existentialist conviction that truth resides in power rather than in ideality, in activity rather than in knowledge.[24] This means that power becomes an evaluative principle, as Johannes de silentio's praise for the strength, courage, and inward intensity of the knight of faith expresses. For both Kierkegaard and Nietzsche, the crucial question facing the existing individual is not an abstract enquiry into the definition of 'the good,' but the question, *how can I become stronger?*

This question can provide a starting point for the philosophy of religion. In order to understand spiritual beliefs and practices in terms of their significance for the individual, we must view them in the context of a task of inward strengthening. Kierkegaard's emphasis on love reminds us that becoming religious involves purifying as well as increasing one's inner power or energy, and that this requires continual receptivity to that which goes beyond, or transcends, the self. As well as inquiring, in the mode of knowledge, about the content of particular doctrines, and attempting to evaluate the 'truth' of this content, we can learn to think philosophically about the ways in which different religious traditions offer techniques for liberation, empowerment, and edification.

Connected to this is the fact, made plain by Kierkegaard's thematization of movement, that existence is characterized by change—and, consequently, by the unknown. Kierkegaard can teach us to approach questions of truth and meaning from this understanding of life as essentially dynamic and open-ended. We have seen how this applies to his interpretation of Christianity: instead of attempting in vain to overcome change by imposing concepts onto the flux of existence, the Christian seeks a different kind of constancy that is *based on movement*. Stability comes not from immobility but from the passionate fidelity that constitutes genuine love: God's love is unceasing *because* it is constantly renewed. Faith allows the Christian to accept and to affirm the changing finite world as grounded in God's constancy.

Kierkegaard's category of repetition, based on his recognition that *becoming* involves both difference and continuity, may facilitate a philosophical approach to comparative studies of religion that is more constructive than mere analysis of doctrines.[25] As Wittgenstein has made clear, religious teachings and beliefs are embedded in a complex of practices, traditions, and language games that make interfaith dialogue very difficult. Given this insight, it may seem to make little sense to place, say, Christianity and Buddhism side by side (whether from the perspective of philosophical enquiry or from the perspective of an individual's spiritual practice). However, Kierkegaard's existential interpretation of Christianity in terms of movement, power, freedom, and so on, could be used to illuminate some of the most essential aspects of Buddhism: for example, the teachings that the apparent solidity and immobility of things is an illusion from which we can liberate ourselves; that a kind of "strengthening of the inner being" is possible through practices such as meditation and ethical restraint; that love (*metta*) is a force capable of transforming destructive habits into a happier, more creative way of living. Perhaps many different forms of religious activity—such as meditation, prayer, confession, reading scriptures, fasting, yoga postures, t'ai chi exercises, singing or chanting, and silence—can be understood in terms of the repeated *purification of inwardness*, where inwardness signifies a sort of movement, power, or energy. This idea of purification is, indeed, central to Kierkegaard's important 1846 discourse on "The Purity of Heart Is to Will One Thing." Kierkegaard may have emphasized the disjunction between the internal and the external for the sake of his attack on Hegel, but there are nevertheless practices, things we *do* in space and time, that are directed toward spiritual upbuilding. The very idea of practice implies repetition. Kierkegaard himself spent half an hour each morning engaged in solitary devotional exercises: according to his servant Westergaard, "he stood up and knelt down a great deal, read aloud, etc."[26] What do these kinds of movements and positions accomplish inwardly—and how? Are there ways of evaluating such practices? What *is* the connection between the internal and the external in this context? These practical questions constitute both the limitation and the legacy of Kierkegaard's inquiry into repetition: his insistence on pure inwardness, his denigration of outward movements and his general lack of interest in the body mean that the day-to-day "how" of religious becoming remains obscure. We can blame this in part on his rather obsessively polemical attitude to Hegelian philosophy, in part on the austerity of Protestant theology, and in part on Kierkegaard's personal resistance to opening and revealing himself to others.

Reading Kierkegaard can teach us, as philosophers and as philosophers of religion, to ask certain questions in order to uncover meanings otherwise concealed. One such question, as Deleuze suggests, asks about what it means to "produce movement." Or, how does the power of becoming express itself? How is the plane of motion grounded? How can a person's life *be true*? Kierkegaard's question of motion may even lead one to ask, *how can I change?* How can I become more loving and kind? How can I live more happily, more truthfully? As the ancient Greeks recognized, movement is a source of wonder: it seems to be such a simple, everyday thing, and yet it raises these profound and difficult questions! We could also reflect here on the ways in which Kierkegaard's writing addresses us as existing individuals, directing us to question our 'powers' of intellectual reflection and our academic pursuits from the perspective of a spiritual mode of valuation—but such questioning is probably best practiced once we have put down our philosophy books.

Notes

Introduction. The Place and the Path

1. Kierkegaard, *Purity of Heart*, p. 84.
2. Kierkegaard, *Concluding Unscientific Postscript*, p. 370 (414).
3. See ibid., pp. 99-100 (109-110).
4. Ibid., p. 377 (421). Jean-Paul Sartre's famous definition of existentialism echoes this: "we believe that *existence* precedes *essence*—or, if you will, that we must begin with the subjective." See Sartre, *Existentialism and Humanism*, p. 26.
5. Ibid., p. 368 (411).

Chapter 1. Metaphysics of Motion

1. Aristotle, *Physics* 191a.
2. Aristotle, *Metaphysics* 991a.
3. Kierkegaard's notes on Schelling's lectures are published in the supplement to the Hong and Hong edition of *The Concept of Irony*. See p. 358.
4. George Stack, "Aristotle and Kierkegaard's Existential Ethics," *Journal of the History of Philosophy* 12 (1974), pp. 1-19. Surprisingly, Stack is the only commentator who gives due recognition to Aristotle's influence on Kierkegaard's interest in movement. According to Stack, "Kierkegaard was quite explicit in regard to his adoption of Aristotle's category of movement. It is . . . the central existential category of his philosophical anthropology . . . it was by virtue of Aristotle's metaphysical categories that Kierkegaard found the Ariadne's thread which enabled him to escape from the necessitarian labyrinth of Hegelian metaphysics." Stack's article also considers some ways in which Kierkegaard's account of choice is implicit in Aristotle's ethical works.
5. *Concluding Unscientific Postscript*, p. 277 (312).
6. Ibid., p. 227 (312).
7. Ibid., p. 387 n. (432 n.).

Chapter 2. The Logic of Becoming

1. See Spinoza, *Ethics*, Part II, L1, L5, L6, L7; Part IV, P39.
2. See Hegel's *Encyclopaedia Logic*, sections 6 and 41.
3. Ibid., section 34.
4. See Hyppolite, *Logic and Existence*, pp. 64; 3.
5. Hegel, *The Philosophical Propaedutic*, p. 168.
6. See Hegel's *Encyclopaedia Logic*, section 81.
7. Ibid., section 119.
8. Hegel, *Phenomenology of Spirit*, sections 534–35. Hegel subsequently uses this analysis of meaning to explain the structure of spirit (*Geist*) itself: "Spirit is not a motionless something, but rather is absolute unrest, pure activity, the negating or ideality of fixed determinations of the understanding . . . not an essence that is already complete before its appearance, keeping within itself behind the host of its appearances, but the essence that is actual in truth only through the determinate forms of its necessary self-revelation." See Hegel's *Philosophy of Spirit*, para. 378. For Hegel, the truth of being is identical with its movement of revelation. Hegel's description of truth as a "circular movement" is echoed in Kierkegaard's concept of repetition, although this abandons the spatial metaphor to express a purely temporal, existential dynamic. Perhaps Heidegger's interpretation of *aletheia* as a process or event of "unconcealment" returns to the Hegelian image of a circular motion within consciousness—although it owes something to Kierkegaard too. Heidegger's philosophical metaphoric of motion will be discussed further in Chapter 9.
9. See Hegel's *Science of Logic*, section 1, ch. 1.

Chapter 3. Kierkegaard's Critique of Hegel

1. *Concluding Unscientific Postscript*, pp. 100n, 101, 107 (111n, 112, 118).
2. *Journals and Papers*, section 1608.
3. Ibid., section 5430.
4. Ibid., section 5388.
5. See Josiah Thompson, *Kierkegaard*, p. 78.
6. *Two Ages*, p. 96.
7. I am indebted to Jon Stewart's translations into English of the key texts of this debate. All my quotations from the Danish sources are his translations, but because these are yet to be published I have given page references to the Danish texts.
8. See Arnold B. Come, *Trendelenburg's Influence on Kierkegaard's Modal Categories*. This excellent monograph discusses Kierkegaard's relationships to both Hegel and Aristotle and engages with philosophical themes that are particularly relevant here, such as freedom and necessity.
9. This comment appears in a draft to *The Concept of Anxiety*: see the supplement to the Hong and Hong edition, p.180.

10. H. L. Martensen, "Rationalism, Supernaturalism and the *principium exclusi medii*," *Tidsskrift for Litteratur og Kritik*, vol. 1 (1839), p. 458.
11. Ibid., p. 465.
12. Mynster, "Review of 'De principio logico exclusi medii inter contradictoria,'" *Tiddskrift for Litteratur og Kritik*, vol. 7, p. 342.
13. Ibid., pp. 345-46; 351.
14. Ibid., p. 352.

Chapter 4. *Either/Or*: Kierkegaard's Principle of Contradiction

1. *Concluding Unscientific Postscript*, p. 226 (252). Subsequent references to Kierkegaard's review of *Either/Or* in the *Postscript* can be found in the appendix to chapter 2, Part 2: "A Glance at a Contemporary Effort in Danish Literature."

Sartre's essay "Kierkegaard: the Singular Universal" discusses Kierkegaard's resistance to Hegel in terms of this opposition between inwardness and knowledge. Sartre comments, for example, on Kierkegaard's "living effort to elude knowledge . . . his claim to be, in his very singularity and at the heart of his finitude, the absolute subject, defined in interiority." See Sartre, *Between Existentialism and Marxism*, pp. 141-169.

2. *Either/Or II*, p. 174 (171).
3. *Either/Or I*, p. 21 (22).
4. *Two Ages*, p. 97.
5. *Either/Or II*, p. 229 (225).
6. *Either/Or 1*, p. 25 (26).
7. Ibid., p. 205 (227).
8. Ibid., p. 35 (37).
9. *Either/Or II*, p. 175 (171).
10. This conversation is recorded by Andreas Schiødte, a contemporary of Kierkegaard. See Bruce H. Kirmmse (ed.), *Encounters with Kierkegaard*, p. 195.
11. *Either/Or II*, p. 180 (176).
12. Ibid., p. 178 (173).
13. Charles Taylor, *Sources of the Self*, p. 450.
14. *Either/Or II*, p. 220 (216).
15. Ibid., p. 227 (223).
16. Ibid., p. 227 (223).
17. Ibid., p. 228 (224).
18. Ibid., pp. 177, 180 (173, 176).
19. Tolstoy uses the same metaphor to describe his life in the 1840s and 1850s, before his marriage and his conversion to Christianity. Chapters 2 and 3 of his autobiographical *Confession* recall a character remarkably similar to Kierkegaard's

aesthete: Tolstoy was also influenced by Hegelian philosophy; he devoted himself to literary pursuits; he became "spiritually ill" and "fell into despair." "My life would come to a standstill, as if I did not know how to live or what to do ... On these occasions ... the same questions always arose: 'Why? What comes next?' ... They fell like full stops, always on the same spot, uniting in one large black spot." *A Confession*, p. 28; see also pp. 22–26.

20. *Either/Or II*, p. 168 (163).

21. In *Being and Nothingness* Sartre, like Judge William, emphasizes the future in connection with freedom and insists that "under no circumstances can the past in any way by itself produce an act." Action, as opposed to mere happening, entails a motive. This motive is a desire to change something, which involves an awareness of non-being, of potentiality: an individual acts freely by projecting himself forward into a future that does not yet exist. Consciousness possesses "the permanent possibility of effecting a breach with its own past." However, it also fears the power of this past—which Sartre describes as "viscosity"—to suck it back from its movement toward the future.

22. *Either/Or II*, p. 174 (171).

23. Ibid., p. 342 (340).

24. Ibid., p. 346 (344).

25. Ibid., p. 351 (349).

27. Ibid., p. 355 (353).

28. Stephen Crites, "Pseudonymous Authorship as Art and as Act," p. 226, published in Josiah Thompson (ed.), *Kierkegaard: A Collection of Critical Essays*. Crites's essay discusses the relationship between the form and content of Kierkegaard's pseudonymous texts, concluding that "the contradiction between the aesthetic medium and the existential import of the book will be resolved when the reader is moved to act: then the book's idea will have found its own medium."

Chapter 5. *Repetition*: The Possibility of Motion

1. *Repetition*, p. 33 (131).

2. Ibid., p. 33 (131).

3. *The Concept of Anxiety*, p. 255.

4. John Caputo offers a similar interpretation of Platonic recollection: "Recollection is the way of immanence. It takes eternity to be a lost possession and time itself to be the source of the loss." See Caputo, "Kierkegaard, Heidegger and the Foundering of Metaphysics," *The International Kierkegaard Commentary on Fear and Trembling and Repetition*, p. 208.

5. *Repetition*, p. 90 (186).

6. Ibid., p. 52 (149).

7. Ibid., p. 33 (131).

8. If we turn to Hegel's writings, we do indeed find echoes of Platonic recollection: in his *Philosophy of Religion* he asserts that "man learns nothing, he only recollects; the truth is something which man originally carries within himself . . . and what has to be done is merely to bring it to consciousness." At the end of the *Phenomenology of Spirit*, Hegel describes the fulfillment of Absolute Spirit in terms of a movement of self-knowing, as "its *withdrawal into itself*" and as "the recollection, the *inwardizing* of [its] experience." See Hegel, *Lectures on the Philosophy of Religion*, 1:165 and 16:160; *The Phenomenology of Spirit*, section 494, pp. 563-64. See also Hyppolite's commentary, *Genesis and Structure of Hegel's Phenomenology of Spirit*, p. 39: "the rise of empirical consciousness to absolute knowledge is possible only if the necessary stages of its ascent are discovered within it. These stages are still within it; all that is needed is to descend into the interiority of memory by an action comparable to Platonic recollection."

9. *Concluding Unscientific Postscript*, p. 194 (217).

10. *Repetition*, p. 52 (148-49).

11. This passage, and all subsequent quotations from Kierkegaard's "Open Letter to Professor Heiberg," can be found in the supplement to the Hong and Hong edition of *Repetition*, pp. 283-319.

12. *Repetition*, p. 52 (149).

13. Ibid., p. 35 (133).

14. See *Repetition*, p. 33 (131), and *Journals and Papers*, 2339, 2367, 3070. For a good summary of Leibniz's influence on Kierkegaard, see Niels Eriksen's *Kierkegaard's Category of Repetition*, pp. 118-19. In *Difference and Repetition*, Deleuze compares Leibniz and Hegel; see pp. 42-51.

15. See Eriksen, *Kierkegaard's Category of Repetition*, p. 119.

16. Again, Leibniz's metaphysics offers an account of identity and difference that seems to anticipate this. In his chapter "What Identity and Diversity Is" in the *New Essays On Human Understanding* (see pp. 229-30), Leibniz argues not only that two beings of the same kind cannot conceivably exist in the same place at the same time, but also that, in addition to this spatiotemporal differentiation, "there must always be an internal *principle of differentiation*: although there can be many things of the same kind, it is still the case that none of them are ever actually alike." Leibniz concludes this discussion by suggesting that individual identity is grounded on a more fundamental differentiation that is integral to existence itself: "What is called the *principle of Individuation* in the Schools, where it is so much enquired after . . . is existence itself, which determines a being to a particular time and place incommunicable to two beings of the same kind. The 'principle of individuation' reduces, in the case of individuals, to the principle of distinction." In elucidating the concept of repetition, Kierkegaard shares with Leibniz his emphasis on an *internal difference* and an *incommunicable singularity* that characterize existing things, as well as his concern to preserve individual freedom while insisting that God's power is the source of all existence.

17. Deleuze, *Difference and Repetition*, p. 1.

18. John Caputo also discusses this connection between repetition and atonement in terms of a movement of actualization: "The highest case of freedom and repetition is the case of the most profound qualitative shift, when the individual emerges as something new, a new person, in the transition from sin to atonement. Atonement is repetition in the highest sense. Sin can only be forgiven, not mediated. This transition is a genuine movement of transcendence in which a prior stage is totally transformed." See Caputo, "Kierkegaard, Heidegger and the Foundering of Metaphysics," *The International Kierkegaard Commentary on Fear and Trembling and Repetition*, p. 212.

19. *The Concept of Anxiety*, p. 90.
20. *Repetition*, p. 90 (186).
21. Ibid., p. 82 (179).
22. Ibid., pp. 123-24 (218).
23. Ibid., p. 91 (187).
24. Ibid., p. 121 (216).
25. Ibid., p. 53 (149).
26. Levinas, "Existence and Ethics," p. 34, in *Kierkegaard: A Critical Reader*, pp. 26-38. Levinas disagrees with Kierkegaard, arguing that the ethical facilitates self-realization: "As a consciousness of a responsibility towards others, the ethical does not disperse us into generality. On the contrary, it individualizes us, treating everyone as a unique individual, a self. Kierkegaard seems to have been unable to recognize this." In the following chapter we will consider Levinas's response to Kierkegaard's interpretation of Abraham.
27. Deleuze, *Difference and Repetition*, p. 3.
28. *Repetition*, p. 126 (221).
29. Ibid., p. 41 (138).
30. Ibid., p. 105 (201).
31. Ibid., p. 42 (139).
32. Ibid., p. 119 (214).
33. In *The Sickness Unto Death* Kierkegaard's pseudonym Anti-Climacus discusses sin in similar terms: "the state of sin . . . becomes the internal intensification of sin, a conscious remaining in the state of sin, so that the law of motion in intensification, here as elsewhere, is inward, in greater and greater intensity of consciousness." See pp. 108-9.
34. For a discussion of the themes of drama and the theater in *Repetition*, see George Pattison, "The Magic Theatre: Drama and Existence in Kierkegaard's *Repetition* and Hesse's *Steppenwolf*" in *The International Kierkegaard Commentary on Fear and Trembling and Repetition*, pp. 359-77. Stephen Crites's section on "The Pseudonymous Theatre" in *Pseudonymous Authorship as Art and as Act*, pp. 215-22, is also interesting.
35. *Repetition*, p. 137 (230).
36. Ibid., p. 134 (228).
37. Deleuze, *Difference and Repetition*, pp. 8-9.

Chapter 6. *Fear and Trembling*: A Higher Plane

1. See supplement to *Fear and Trembling*, p. 243.
2. *Journals and Papers*, 2383.
3. *Fear and Trembling*, p. 3.
4. Ibid., p. 3.
5. Ibid., p. 69.
6. Ibid., p. 42 n.
7. *Concluding Unscientific Postscript*, p. 103 (113).
8. *Fear and Trembling*, p. 46.
9. Ibid., p. 69.
10. Ibid., p. 69.
11. Ibid., p. 121.
12. Ibid., p. 9.
13. Ibid., p. 33.
14. Ibid., p. 38.
15. Ibid., p. 41.
16. Ibid., p. 45.
17. Ibid., p. 119.
18. Ibid., p. 44.
19. Ibid., p. 35.
20. Ibid., p. 43.
21. Ibid., pp. 42-43. Commenting on this passage, Stephen Crites highlights the elements of movement and power that constitute the individual's inward "concentration": "faith is a single unconditional passion, the *momentum* of which draws the dissipated *energies* and fragmentary possibilities of the self into a unity"; see Crites, "Pseudonymous Authorship as Art and as Act" in *Kierkegaard. A Collection of Critical Essays*, p. 193.
22. Ibid., pp. 50; 47.
23. Ibid., p. 44.
24. Ibid., p. 48.
25. *Works of Love*, p. 349. Don Cupitt has suggested that Nietzsche's proclamation of the death of God may be interpreted in the light of this remark, as making possible a purer, more spiritual form of religion. Nietzsche describes churches as the tombs of a dead God—but, says Cupitt, why shouldn't we go to church and worship God just as we visit graves to talk to our beloved? Might not a prayer that expects no response be less self-concerned than one that is motivated by hope of a result?
26. *Fear and Trembling*, p. 101.
27. Ibid., p. 41.
28. This is crucial in the context of the Christian gospel's proclamation of a shift from law to love as the basis for faith. Of course, this has been a controversial issue throughout the history of Christian theology; for a helpful summary

of the debate about Kierkegaard's position see Gouwens, *Kierkegaard as Religious Thinker*, pp. 188–92.

29. Jacques Derrida emphasizes *Fear and Trembling*'s rejection of the generality of ethics. He argues that Abraham's sacrifice teaches us that "far from ensuring responsibility, the generality of ethics incites to irresponsibility. It impels me to speak, to reply, to account for something, and thus to dissolve my singularity in the medium of the concept. Such is the aporia of responsibility . . . For responsibility . . . demands on the one hand an accounting, a general answering-for-oneself with respect to the general and before the generality, hence the idea of substitution, and, on the other hand, uniqueness, absolute singularity, hence nonsubstitution, nonrepetition, silence and secrecy." See Derrida, *The Gift of Death*, p. 61. Although Derrida's analysis is original and thought provoking, he seems to be rather confused about the meaning of repetition. While Deleuze emphasizes that repetition is opposed to generality, Derrida *identifies* repetition with generality; see also his reference to "the generality or the repetition of the same," p. 84.

Emmanuel Levinas disagrees with Derrida, and with Kierkegaard, about the question of responsibility, arguing that "it is only in the ethical that an appeal can be made to the singularity of the subject." Levinas disputes Kierkegaard's interpretation of Abraham as exemplifying the raising of subjectivity above the ethical law: "The opposite interpretation is also possible: the highest point of the whole drama may be the moment when Abraham paused and listened to the voice that would lead him back to the ethical order by commanding him not to commit a human sacrifice." See Levinas, "Existence and Ethics," in *Kierkegaard: A Critical Reader*, p. 34. The disagreement here seems to be due primarily to divergent interpretations of the ethical, rather than of Abraham: because Levinas views God as synonymous with the ethical, he finds that Abraham's situation does not represent a conflict with ethics. For Kierkegaard, however, the ethical is a human sphere from which God, as transcendent, is absolutely distinct; this means that, whether or not the divine command is ethically acceptable, Abraham's obedience raises him above the ethical *as an end in itself*.

30. *Fear and Trembling*, p. 48.

31. I must clarify the meaning of immanence here, for it may be applied to Kierkegaard in at least two senses. In the narrower sense, immanence refers to the domain of rationality, of conceptual reflection: this is the immanence that Kierkegaard associates with Hegelian philosophy, and which, he claims, is incapable of producing any movement. This immanence is constituted by necessity; it is defined in opposition to existence and its freedom. So in this sense, human existence always breaks with immanence; its self-actualization continually produces the new. On the other hand, in its wider sense immanence refers to the entire human, worldly realm, to the extent of human powers; as such, it stands opposed to transcendence, which means the actualization of *God*'s power. It is in this second sense that infinite resignation represents the greatest immanent movement.

32. *Fear and Trembling*, p. 34.

33. Ibid., p. 120.
34. Ibid., p. 37.
35. Ibid., p. 104.
36. Ibid., p. 50.
37. The leap is one of Kierkegaard's most familiar categories and is much discussed by his commentators. Kierkegaard's leap is to some extent influenced by Lessing, although in these 1843 texts none of the occasional references to Lessing concern transitions or movements; see *Fear and Trembling*, pp. 67, 88; and *Repetition*, p. 141. (Ronald M. Green argues that Kierkegaard owes his concept of the leap more to Kant than to Lessing; see Green, *Kierkegaard and Kant: The Hidden Debt*.) The Hongs' note on the leap simply states that "the concept of the leap pertains to qualitative transitions, which cannot be accounted for by quantitative changes or by Hegelian mediation." The leap echoes Aristotle's concept of kinesis, for Kierkegaard says that the change from possibility to actuality is a leap; see *Concluding Unscientific Postscript*, p. 342; *Journals and Papers* 109-10. He also links this to Christianity, where "the central issue is a qualitative transformation, a total character transformation in time (just as qualitative as the change from not being to being which is birth). Anything which is merely a development of what man is originally is not essentially Christian"; see *Journals and Papers*, 3101, and also 261, 2358.
38. One relevant variation of this transition appears in the *Philosophical Fragments*, where Climacus discusses rational proofs of the existence of God: "how does the existence of the God emerge from the demonstration?—I have to let go of it . . . Yet this letting go, even that is surely something; it is, after all, my contribution. Does it not have to be taken into account, this diminutive moment, however brief it is—it does not have to be long, because it is a leap." See p. 42 (33). Climacus later describes the leap to Christian faith as a "qualitative" transition and a "break in immanence"; see *Concluding Unscientific Postscript*, pp. 12, 95, 103, 381.
39. *Journals and Papers* 2352; *Concluding Unscientific Postscript*, p. 99, 92 (109, 99)
40. *Fear and Trembling*, p. 42. To this remark Johannes adds an obscure reference to a poem that ends with the line *ein seliger Sprung in die Ewigkeit*, "a blessed leap into eternity."
41. Ibid., p. 49
42. *Concluding Unscientific Postscript*, p. 112 (124).
43. Ibid., pp. 201, 370, 188 (224, 385, 199).
44. Deleuze, *Difference and Repetition*, p. 1. Similarly, Derrida suggests that "absolute duty (towards God and in the singularity of faith) implies a sort of gift or sacrifice that functions beyond both debt and duty, beyond duty as a form of debt. This is the dimension that provides for a 'gift of death' which, beyond human responsibility, beyond the universal concept of duty, is a response to absolute duty"; Derrida, ibid., p. 63. A fascinating question here is how this relates to the sacrifice of Jesus; see Derrida on the Gospel of Matthew, ibid., pp. 88-110.

45. *Fear and Trembling*, p. 34.

46. Simone Weil uses metaphors of movement in her writings about grace, which have rather Kierkegaardian resonances: "To come down by a movement in which gravity plays no part. Gravity makes things come down, wings make them rise: what wings raised to the second power can make things come down without weight? . . . Grace is the law of the descending movement." See Weil, *Gravity and Grace*, pp. 3-4.

47. As Louis Dupre suggests, "Grace constitutes a relationship, and a relationship cannot exist without two *real* terms. Only God can bring about this relationship, but even He is powerless if man, the other term involved, does not choose with all his force to accept God's causal activity . . . As the meeting point of God and man, faith is at once divine grace and the highest human activity." See Dupre, *Kierkegaard as Theologian*, pp. 107, 97. Perhaps because of the central role of love in the question of the relationship between freedom and transcendence, Dupre's theological approach provides a clear interpretation of Kierkegaard's position. He argues that Kierkegaard is "someone who takes Christianity's claims of transcendence seriously . . . his dialectic is not autonomous but is determined at every moment by transcendent categories"; on the other hand, "one of [Kierkegaard's] most significant conclusions is the recognition of the role that freedom plays in the acceptance of faith and grace"; pp. x-xiii. Focusing on the theme of love, Sylvia Walsh makes a similar point: "Kierkegaard takes seriously the identity of God as the transcendent ground of love, thus opening the way for the working out of a relational rather than a substantive understanding of the divine"; see Walsh, "Forming the Heart: The Role of Love in Kierkegaard's Thought," in *The Grammar of the Heart*, ed. Bell, pp. 243-56; p. 249.

More philosophical analyses of these issues tend to find the balance between freedom and transcendence problematic; see, for example, Timothy P. Jackson, "Arminian Edification: Kierkegaard on Grace and Free Will" in *The Cambridge Companion to Kierkegaard*, pp. 235-56; Michelle Kosch, "Freedom and Immanence," in *Kierkegaard and Freedom*, ed. Giles, pp. 121-41; Terence Penelhum, *God and Skepticism: A Study in Skepticism and Fideism*, p. 83. M. Jamie Ferreira's *Transforming Vision* argues that faith is neither an act of willpower, nor a miracle of grace; instead, Ferreira interprets the Kierkegaardian leap as a shift in perspective, as an imaginative activity. Similarly, Charles Taylor finds in post-Romantic thinkers such as Kierkegaard an emphasis on "a transformation of our own vision, rather than simply . . . a recognition of some objective order of goodness"; see Taylor, *Sources of the Self*, p. 448. I would argue that Ferreira and Taylor do not give enough weight to Kierkegaard's insistence on transcendence.

48. This refers to the position exemplified by Don Cupitt, who argues that a Christian life may be lived without belief in an objective God. "Nonrealism" has inspired much debate in recent years among practising Christians as well as academic theologians and philosophers of religion. As a thoughtful, creative response to philosophers such as Nietzsche, Heidegger, and Wittgenstien, Cupitt's religious

writing raises profound questions concerning religious faith—but it would be a mistake to interpret Kierkegaardian faith as belonging to subjectivity in any sense that opposes the transcendent power of God. As Cupitt recognizes, nonrealism and immanence go together, and this excludes Kierkegaard's position.

With reference to the *Postscript*, C. Stephen Evans discusses the seemingly puzzling fact that Kierkegaard emphasizes both subjectivity and belief in "an objective mind-independent reality," and comments on Richard Rorty's antirealism in *Philosophy and the Mirror of Nature*. Evans concludes that objective reality "is part of the structure of 'belief' or 'faith' . . . The mind-independent character of reality is precisely what gives belief its risky character"; see Evans, "Realism and Anti-realism in the *Postscript*," in *The Cambridge Companion to Kierkegaard*, pp. 154–76; pp. 169–71.

49. *Fear and Trembling*, pp. 50, 39.
50. Ibid., p. 34.
51. Spinoza, *Ethics* III, P11 schol.; IV preface.
52. Nietzsche, *The Will to Power*, pp. 485 (fragment 917); 366 (fragment 688). See also Heidegger's lectures on *The Will to Power*, published as *Nietzsche*, especially pp. 35–53. Commenting on the passage cited above, Heidegger remarks that "this 'consciousness of difference' . . . is not knowledge in the sense of mere representation and cognition. Joy . . . is something that brings us to ourselves, not by way of knowledge but by way of feeling, by way of an away-beyond us . . . the disparity implied in being out beyond ourselves is first opened up and given form by joy."

Chapter 7. Becoming a Christian

1. *Journals and Papers*, 6346, 6535.
2. *Fighteen Upbuilding Discourses*, p. 5.
3. Ibid., p. 107.
4. See Kierkegaard's *For Self-Examination* for an in-depth discussion of the significance of James. I am indebted to Hugh Pyper's comments on this aspect of Kierkegaard's thought, and direct readers to Pyper's fascinating article on the connection between the Epistle of James and *The Concept of Anxiety*, "Adam's Angest. The Myth of Language and the Language of Mythology," *Kierkegaard Studies Yearbook 2001*, eds. Cappelhorn, Deuser and Stewart, pp. 78–95.
5. *Eighteen Upbuilding Discourses*, p. 138. See also p. 173.
6. Ibid., p. 133.
7. Ibid., pp. 172; 174.
8. Ibid., p. 134.
9. Ibid., pp. 170–1.
10. Ibid., p. 83.
11. Ibid., pp. 86–7.
12. Ibid., p. 107.

13. Ibid., p. 60.

14. Ibid., p. 61.

15. Nicholas Berdyaev describes this vertical axis of spiritual movement in terms very reminiscent of Kierkegaard, emphasizing the opposition between freedom and necessity that motivates Kierkegaard's polemic against Hegelian philosophy: "The human spirit is in prison. Prison is what I call this given world of necessity . . . And the true way is that of spiritual liberation from 'the world,' the liberation of man's spirit from its bondage to necessity. The true way is not a movement to the right or left in the plane of 'the world,' but rather movement upward and downward on the lines of the ultra-worldly, movement in spirit and not in 'the world.'" See Berdyaev, *The Meaning of the Creative Act*, p. 11. As this title suggests, Berdyaev's existentialist interpretation of Christianity explores the themes of power and activity that are so central to Kierkegaard's thought.

16. *The Point of View for My Work as an Author*, p. 497. See also the Hongs' introduction to *Eighteen Upbuilding Discourses*, p. xiii.

17. See the supplement to *Eighteen Upbuilding Discourses*, p. 489, and also the Introduction, pp. xiv-xvi.

18. *Philosophical Fragments*, pp. 15, 23 (12, 19).

19. Ibid., pp. 93 (75).

20. Ibid., p. 30 (24).

21. Ibid., p. 38 (30).

22. *The Concept of Anxiety*, p. 21.

23. Ibid., pp. 11-13.

24. *The Sickness Unto Death*, pp. 108-9.

Chapter 8. Beyond Philosophy?

1. Following John Caputo's interpretation of repetition's disruption of metaphysics in the context of the "event of nihilism" subsequently proclaimed by Nietzsche and Heidegger, Niels Eriksen suggests that Kierkegaard's Christian perspective has much to offer philosophy. "Kierkegaard turns the Christian teaching of the Incarnation against metaphysics . . . the Incarnation thus becomes a paradigm for post-metaphysical thinking"; see Eriksen, *Kierkegaard's Category of Repetition*. (Mark C. Taylor makes a similar point, inspired by Derrida, in *Erring: A Post-Modern A-Theology*, although with a more theological emphasis.) There is a question here about whether this "post-metaphysical thinking" could be meaningful only in a Christian context, and perhaps we should be wary of treating Kierkegaard's interpretations of Christian teachings as intellectual paradigms, since they are supposed to be existential paradigms.

2. Phillip Cary, *Augustine's Invention of the Inner Self*, p. 67. This historical study of Augustine, which focuses on the theme of inwardness, is interesting to consider alongside our interpretation of Kierkegaard.

3. *Concluding Unscientific Postscript*, p. 51 (52).
4. Ibid., p. 100 (110).
5. Ibid., p. 107-8, 133 (118-9, 149).
6. Ibid., p. 282 (318).
7. This remark was made in conversation with M. O'C. Drury. See Rush Rhees (ed.), *Ludvig Wittgenstein: Personal Recollections*, p. 120.
8. Don Cupitt offers a similarly aesthetic interpretation of religious and philosophical thought and emphasizes the irreducibility of language. Recently he has used the term "brightness" to describe the way language lights up the world: see his *Emptiness and Brightness*. This is very far from a Kierkegaardian position, in that the self is fully expressive and has no inwardness: Cupitt's view that the mind is "out there," spread over the world, echoes Husserl's phenomenological interpretation of consciousness as characterized by movements of "intentionality."
9. Deleuze, *Spinoza: Practical Philosophy*, p. 98.

Chapter 9. Repetitions

1. Nietzsche, *The Will to Power*, p. 492.
2. Here, "ethical" signifies neither morality nor Kierkegaard's ethical sphere, but rather an existential kind of truth.
3. Nietzsche, *The Will to Power*, p. 295.
4. Nietzsche, *On the Genealogy of Morals*, p. 45 (first essay, section 13).
5. Niels Eriksen offers a similar comparison between Kierkegaard and Nietzsche: "while they share the view that the concept of repetition indicates the way out of the realm of Platonic metaphysics, they sought this exit in opposite extremes of that realm . . . Kierkegaardian repetition assuming the absolute otherness of the eternal, and Nietzschean recurrence abolishing any genuine otherness." See Eriksen, *Kierkegaard's Category of Repetition*, p. 154; also pp. 136-64.
6. Deleuze, *Difference and Repetition*, p. 5.
7. Ibid., p. 8.
8. Ibid., pp. 10-11.
9. Ibid., p. 295.
10. Heidegger, *Being and Time*, p. 427. See also *On Time and Being*, pp. 14-15.
11. Ibid., p. 444. George Pattison has offered a rather Heideggerian interpretation of *Repetition*, which recognizes the significance of the concept of kinesis, and considers the difference integral to repetition in terms of a dual relationship to the future and "the Other." "The sustaining heartbeat of Kierkegaard's small masterpiece *Repetition* is the quest/question concerning the realization of a genuine openness to the future that is at the same time a genuine openness to the Other . . . [F]or Kierkegaard's thought as a whole (and for later existentialist philosophy) the future and the Other are the two fundamental ecstasies of the self in relation to which the self first acquires the character of a fully individual identity.

In the vocabulary of classical philosophy (which is the point of departure for *Repetition*) they are the primary modes of motion, change or *kinesis* as these are represented within the horizon of a post-Cartesian philosophy." See Pattison, "The Magic Theatre: Drama and Existence in Kierkegaard's *Repetition* and Hesse's *Steppenwolf*," in the *International Kierkegaard Commentary on* Fear and Trembling *and* Repetition, pp. 359-77.

12. In his excellent biography of Heidegger, Rudiger Safranski discusses this application of the phenomenological method to religious questions: "Heidegger speaks of God as Husserl does of reality outside consciousness. Husserl brackets reality in; Heidegger brackets God in." See Safranski, *Martin Heidegger*, pp. 107-12.

13. Heidegger, *Being and Time*, p. 444.

14. Heidegger, "The End of Philosophy and the Task of Thinking," *Basic Writings*, pp. 441-43.

15. Heidegger, "The Origin of the Work of Art," *Basic Writings* p. 196.

16. Deleuze, *Difference and Repetition*, p. 65.

17. Heidegger, *Being and Time*, p. 494.

18. Heidegger, "The End of Philosophy and the Task of Thinking," *Basic Writings*, p. 436.

19. Ibid., p. 449.

20. Heidegger, *Discourse on Thinking*, pp. 69-70.

21. See Nietzsche, *The Gay Science*, p. 181 (section 125).

22. Sartre, *Nausea*, pp. 190-91.

23. Sylvia Walsh emphasizes the importance of this aspect of Kierkegaard's project in the light of a tendency among philosophers to avoid engaging with the issue of love—see Walsh, "Forming the Heart: The Role of Love in Kierkegaard's Thought," *The Grammar of the Heart* ed. Richard Bell, pp. 234-56. Irving Singer makes this point more generally, arguing that "in the last sixty years or so the analysis of love has been neglected more than almost any other subject in philosophy"; see Singer, *The Nature of Love*, vol. 1, p. xi.

24. Sartre, *Existentialism And Humanism*, p. 26.

25. Keith Yandell's philosophy of religions, for example, begins by examining the different ontological claims of religious traditions and argues that these traditions, to the extent to which they diverge, are incommensurable. Yandell's argument that any suggestion that all religions are essentially the same is certainly convincing, but his approach leads to the problematic suggestion that at least some religious teachings must be wrong. See Yandell, *Philosophy of Religion: A Contemporary Introduction*.

26. See Bruce H. Kirmmse (ed.), *Encounters with Kierkegaard*, p. 195.

Bibliography

Works by Kierkegaard

Either/Or (two volumes). Trans. David F. Swenson and Lilian Marvin Swenson. New York: Doubleday (Anchor Books) 1959.

Repetition. Trans. Walter Lowrie. New York: Harper and Row, 1964.

Fear and Trembling. Trans. Hong and Hong. Princeton: Princeton University Press, 1983.

Philosophical Fragments. Trans. David F. Swenson, Princeton: Princeton University Press, 1962.

The Concept of Anxiety. Trans. and ed. Reidar Thomte and Albert B. Anderson. Princeton: Princeton University Press, 1980.

Concluding Unscientific Postscript. Trans. David F. Swenson and Walter Lowrie. Princeton: Princeton University Press, 1941.

The Sickness Unto Death. Trans. Hong and Hong. Princeton: Princeton University Press, 1980.

The Concept of Irony. Trans. Hong and Hong. Princeton: Princeton University Press, 1989.

Eighteen Upbuilding Discourses. Trans. Hong and Hong. Princeton: Princeton University Press, 1990.

Works of Love. Trans. Hong and Hong. Princeton: Princeton University Press, 1988.

Journals and Papers (seven volumes). Trans. Hong and Hong. Princeton: Princeton University Press, 1967-1978.

Purity of Heart Is To Will One Thing. Trans. Douglas V. Steere. New York: Harper and Row, 1956.

Secondary Literature about Kierkegaard

Adorno. Theodor. *Kierkegaard: Construction of the Aesthetic.* Trans. and ed. Robert Hullot-Kentor. Minneapolis: University of Minnesota Press, 1989.

Agacinski, Sylviane. "We Are Not Sublime: Love and Sacrifice, Abraham and Ourselves", in *Kierkegaard: A Critical Reader.* Ed. Jonathan Rée and Jane Chamberlain. Oxford: Blackwell, 1998.

Blanchette, Olivia. "The Silencing of Philosophy." In *The International Kierkegaard Commentary* on Fear and Trembling *and* Repetition. E. Robert L. Perkins. Macon, GA: Mercer University Press, 1993.

Caputo, John D. *Radical Hermeneutics.* Bloomington: Indiana University Press, 1987.

———. "Kierkegaard, Heidegger and the Foundering of Metaphysics." In *The International Kierkegaard Commentary* on Fear and Trembling *and* Repetition. Ed. Robert L. Perkins. Macon, GA: Mercer University Press, 1993.

Come, Arnold B. *Trendelenburg's Influence on Kierkegaard's Modal Categories.* Montreal: Inter Editions, 1991.

Crites, Stephen. "Pseudonymous Authorship as Art and as Act." In *Kierkegaard: A Collection of Critical Essays.* Ed. Josiah Thompson. New York: Doubleday (Anchor Books), 1972.

Derrida, Jaques. *The Gift of Death.* Chicago: University of Chicago Press, 1995.

Dunning, Stephen N. *Kierkegaard's Dialectic of Inwardness.* Princeton: Princeton University Press, 1985.

Dupré, Louis. *Kierkegaard as Theologian.* New York: Sheed and Ward, 1963.

Eriksen, Niels Nyman. *Kierkegaard's Category of Repetition.* Berlin and New York: Walter de Gruyter, 2000.

Evans, C. Stephen. "Realism and Anti-Realism in the *Postscript.*" In *The Cambridge Companion to Kierkegaard.* Ed. Alastair Hannay and Gordon D. Marino. Cambridge: Cambridge University Press, 1998.

Ferreira, M. Jamie. *Transforming Vision, Imagination and Will in Kierkegaardian Faith.* Oxford: Oxford University Press, 1991.

——— . "Faith and the Kierkegaardian Leap." In *The Cambridge Companion to Kierkegaard*. Ed. Alastair Hannay and Gordon D. Marino. Cambridge: Cambridge University Press, 1998.

Green, Ronald M. *Kierkegaard and Kant: The Hidden Debt*. Albany: State University of New York Press, 1992.

Gouwens, David J. *Kierkegaard as Religious Thinker*. Cambridge: Cambridge University Press, 1996.

Hannay, Alastair. *Kierkegaard*. London: Routledge, 1991.

Jackson, Timothy P., "Arminian Edification: Kierkegaard on Grace and Free Will", *The Cambridge Companion to Kierkegaard*. Ed. Alastair Hannay and Gordon D. Marino. Cambridge: Cambridge University Press, 1998.

Keeley, Louise Carroll. "The Parables of Problem III in Kierkegaard's *Fear and Trembling*." In *The International Kierkegaard Commentary on Fear and Trembling and Repetition*. Ed. Robert L. Perkins. Macon, GA: Mercer University Press, 1993.

Kellenberger, J. *Kierkegaard and Nietzsche*. Basingstoke: Macmillan, 1997.

Kirmmse, Bruce H. (ed.). *Encounters with Kierkegaard: A Life as Seen by His Contemporaries*. Princeton: Princeton University Press, 1996.

Kosch, Michelle. "Freedom and Immanence." In *Kierkegaard and Freedom*. Ed. James Giles. Basingstoke: Palgrave, 2000.

Law, David R. "The Place, Role and Function of the 'Ultimatum' of *Either/Or*, Part Two, in Kierkegaard's Pseudonymous Authorship"; and "The 'Ultimatum' of Kierkegaard's *Either/Or*, Part Two, and the *Two Upbuilding Discourses* of 16 May 1843." In *The International Kierkegaard Commentary on Either/Or, Volume 2*. Ed. Robert L. Perkins. Macon, GA: Mercer University Press, 1995.

Levinas, Emmanuel. "Existence and Ethics." In *Kierkegaard: A Critical Reader*. Ed. Jonathan Rée and Jane Chamberlain. Oxford: Blackwell, 1998.

Mackey, Louis. *Kierkegaard: A Kind of Poet*. Philadelphia: University of Pennsylvania Press, 1971.

Mooney, Edward F. *Selves in Discord and Resolve*. London: Routledge, 1996.

——— . "Art, Deed and System: The Prefaces to *Fear and Trembling*." In *The International Kierkegaard Commentary on Fear and Trembling and Repetition*. Ed. Robert L. Perkins. Macon, GA: Mercer University Press, 1993.

Pattison, George. "The Magic Theatre: Drama and Existence in Kierkegaard's *Repetition* and Hesse's *Steppenwolf*." In *The International Kierkegaard Commentary on Fear and Trembling and Repetition*. Ed. Robert L. Perkins. Macon, GA: Mercer University Press, 1993.

——. "The Initial Reception of *Either/Or*." In *The International Kierkegaard Commentary on Either/Or, Volume 2*. Ed. Robert L. Perkins. Macon, GA: Mercer University Press, 1995.

Perkins, Robert L. "Either/Or/Or: Giving the Parson His Due." In *The International Kierkegaard Commentary on Either/Or, Volume 2*. Ed. Robert L. Perkins. Macon, GA: Mercer University Press, 1995.

Pojman, Louis. "Kierkegaard's Phenomenology of the Stages of Existence." In *Faith, Knowledge and Action: Essays to Niels Thulstrup*. Ed. G.L. Stengren. Copenhagen: C. A. Reitzels, 1984.

Pyper, Hugh. "Adam's Angest: The Myth of Language and the Language of Mythology." *Kierkegaard Studies Yearbook 2001*. Eds. N. J. Cappelhorn, H. Deuser, J. Stewart. Berlin: Walter de Gruyter, 2001.

Ricoeur, Paul. "Philosophy after Kierkegaard." In *Kierkegaard: A Critical Reader*. Ed. Jonathan Rée and Jane Chamberlain. Oxford: Blackwell, 1998.

Stack, George. "Aristotle and Kierkegaard's Existential Ethics." In *Journal of the History of Philosophy* 12, 1974.

Sussman, Henry. *The Hegelian Aftermath*. Baltimore: John Hopkins University Press, 1982.

Thulstrup, Niels. *Kierkegaard's Relation to Hegel*. Trans. George L. Stengren. Princeton: Princeton University Press, 1980.

Taylor, Mark. C. *Journeys to Selfhood: Kierkegaard and Hegel*. Los Angeles: University of California Press, 1980.

Thompson, Josiah. *Kierkegaard*. New York: Knopf, 1973.

Wahl, Jean. "Hegel et Kierkegaard." *Revue philosophique de la France et de l'étranger* 112, 1931.

Walsh, Sylvia I. "Forming the Heart: The Role of Love in Kierkegaard's Thought." In *The Grammar of the Heart*. Ed. Richard H. Bell. San Francisco: Harper and Row, 1988.

Westphal, Merold. "Kierkegaard and Hegel." In *The Cambridge Companion to Kierkegaard*. Ed. Alastair Hannay and Gordon D. Marino. Cambridge: Cambridge University Press, 1998.

Other Texts

Allan, D. J. *The Philosophy of Aristotle*. Oxford: Oxford University Press, 1952.

Aristotle. *The Complete Works Of Aristotle* (two volumes). Ed. Jonathan Barnes. Princeton: Princeton University Press, 1984.

Augustine. *Confessions*. New York: Penguin, 1961.

Barnes, Jonathan. *Aristotle*. Cambridge: Cambridge University Press, 1982.

Berdyaev, Nicholas. *The Meaning of the Creative Act*. Trans. Donald A. Lowrie. London: Victor Gollancz, 1955.

Cary, Phillip. *Augustine's Invention of the Inner Self*. Oxford: Oxford University Press, 2000.

Cupitt, Don. *The Sea of Faith*. London: SCM, 1994.

——. *Solar Ethics*. London: SCM Press, 1995.

——. *Emptiness and Brightness*. Santa Rosa, CA: Polebridge, 2001.

Deleuze, Gilles. *Difference and Repetition*. Trans. Paul Patton. London: Athlone, 1994.

——. *Kant's Critical Philosophy*. Trans. Hugh Tomlinson and Barbara Habberjam. London: Athlone, 1995.

——. *Spinoza: Practical Philosophy*. Trans. Robert Hurley. San Francisco: City Lights Books, 1988.

——, and Felix Guattari. *What Is Philosophy?* Trans. Hugh Tomlinson and Graham Burchill. London and New York: Verso, 1994.

Guthrie, W. K. C. *A History of Greek Philosophy, Vol. Six: Aristotle–An Encounter*. Cambridge: Cambridge University Press, 1981.

Hegel, G. W. F. *The Phenomenology of Spirit*. Trans. A.V. Miller. Oxford: Oxford University Press, 1977.

——. *Hegel's Logic (Being Part I of the Encyclopaedia . . .)*. Trans. William Wallace. Oxford: Oxford University Press, 1975.

——. *The Philosophical Propadeutic*. Trans. A.V. Miller. Oxford: Blackwell, 1986.

——. *Philosophy of Nature*. Trans. A.V. Miller. Oxford: Oxford University Press, 1970.

——. *Early Theological Writings*. Trans. T. M. Knox. Chicago: University of Chicago Press, 1948.

―――. *Faith and Knowledge*. Trans. and ed. W. Cerf and H. S. Harris. Albany: State University of New York Press, 1977.

―――. *Lectures on the Philosophy of Religion* (three volumes). Trans. E. B. Speirs and J. B. Sanderson. London: Routledge and Kegan Paul, 1962.

―――. *The Hegel Reader*. Ed. Stephen Houlgate. Oxford: Blackwell, 1998.

Heidegger, Martin. *Being and Time*. Trans. John Macquarrie and Edward Robinson. Oxford: Blackwell, 1962.

―――. *Basic Writings*. Ed. David Farrell Krell. London: Routledge, 1993.

―――. *On Time and Being*. Trans. Joan Stambaugh. New York: Harper and Row, 1972.

―――. *Nietzsche*. Trans. David Farrell Krell. New York: Harper Collins, 1991.

―――. *Discourse on Thinking*. Trans. John M. Anderson and E. Hans Freund. New York: Harper and Row, 1966.

Heraclitus. *Fragments*. Trans. T. M. Robinson. Toronto: University of Toronto Press, 1987.

Hobbes, Thomas. *Leviathan*. Chicago: Aldine, 1953.

―――. *Thomas White's De Mundo Examined*. Trans. Harold Whitmore Jones. London: Bedford University Press, 1976.

Hyppolite, Jean. *Logic and Existence*. Trans. Leonard Lawlor and Amit Sen. Albany: State University of New York Press, 1997.

―――. *Genesis and Structure of Hegel's Phenomenology of Spirit*. Trans. S. Cherniak and J. Heckman. Evanston: Northwestern University Press, 1974.

Kant, Immanuel. *Critique of Pure Reason*. Trans. Norman Kemp Smith. London: Macmillan, 1929.

Kojève, A. *Introduction to the Reading of Hegel: Lectures on the "Phenomenology of Spirit."* Trans. J. H. Nicholls. Ithaca: Cornell University Press, 1980.

Kosman, Aryeh. "Aristotle's Prime Mover." In *Self-Motion from Aristotle to Newton*. Ed. Mary Louise Gill and James G. Lennox, Princeton University Press, 1994.

Leibniz, G. W. *Philosophical Essays*. Trans. Roger Ariew and Daniel Garber. Indianapolis: Hackett, 1989.

―――. *New Essays on Human Understanding*. Trans. and ed. P. Remnant and J. Bennet. Cambridge: Cambridge University Press, 1982.

Lowith, Karl. *Martin Heidegger and European Nihilism*. Trans. Gary Steiner. New York: Columbia University Press, 1995.

Martinich, A. P. *A Hobbes Dictionary*. Oxford: Blackwell, 1995.

Merleau-Ponty, Maurice. *Sense and Non-Sense*. Evanston: Northwestern University Press, 1964.

Nietzsche, Friedrich. *On The Genealogy of Morals*. Trans. Walter Kaufmann. New York: Vintage Books, 1967.

——. *The Gay Science*. Trans. Walter Kaufmann. New York: Vintage, 1974.

——. *Thus Spoke Zarathustra*. Trans. R. J Hollingdale. New York: Penguin, 1969.

——. *The Will to Power*. Trans. Walter Kaufmann and R. J. Hollingdale. New York: Vintage, 1968.

Penelhum, Terence. *God and Skepticism: A Study in Skepticism and Fideism*. Dordrecht: Reidel, 1983.

Plato. *The Dialogues of Plato* (four volumes). Trans. B. Jowett. Oxford: Oxford University Press, 1953.

Rhees, Rush (ed.). *Ludvig Wittgenstein: Personal Recollections*. Oxford: Blackwell, 1981.

Ross, Sir David. *Aristotle*. London: Methuen, 1923.

Safranski, Rüdiger. *Martin Heidegger*. Trans. Ewald Osers. Cambridge: Harvard University Press, 1998.

Sartre, Jean-Paul. *Being and Nothingness*. Trans. Hazel E. Barnes. London: Methuen, 1958.

——. *Between Existentialism and Marxism*. Trans. John Matthews. London: New Left Books, 1974.

——. *Existentialism and Humanism*. Trans. Philip Mairet. London: Methuen, 1948.

——. *Nausea*. Trans. Robert Baldick. Middlesex: Penguin, 1965.

Singer, Irving. *The Nature of Love* vol. 1, Chicago: University of Chicago Press, 1984.

Sorabji, Richard. *Matter, Space and Motion*. London: Duckworth, 1988.

Spinoza, Benedict de. *Ethics*. Trans. Edwin Curley. London: Penguin, 1996.

Taylor, Charles. *Sources of the Self*. Cambridge: Cambridge University Press, 1989.

Tolstoy, Leo. *A Confession and Other Religious Writings*. Trans. Jane Kentish. London: Penguin, 1987.

Warnock, Mary. *Existentialism*. Oxford: Oxford University Press, 1970.

Waterlow, Sarah. *Nature, Change and Agency in Aristotle's Physics*. Oxford: Oxford University Press, 1982.

Weil, Simone. *Gravity and Grace*. Trans. Emma Craufurd. London: Routledge, 1963.

Wittgenstein, Ludwig. *The Blue and Brown Books*. New York: Harper and Row, 1965.

Zizek, Slavoj. *The Abyss of Freedom*. Ann Arbor: University of Michigan Press, 1997.

——— . *The Plague of Fantasies*. London Verso, 1997.

Index

Abraham, 91-100, 105, 107, 110, 113, 156
absurd, the, 106-9, 144
academia, 33-34, 38-39, 55, 130-31, 148
acceptance (of finite existence), 105, 117
actuality, 12-13, 15
actualization. *See* kinesis
Adam and Eve, 123-24
aesthetic existence, 38, 51-63, 95, 113, 138
aesthetics (Kantian), 131-32
Anselm, 23
Aquinas, 23
Aristotle, 4, 9, 11-23, 25, 27, 33, 40, 52, 56, 59, 72-74, 82, 122-23, 128, 145, 149
art, philosophy as, 133
atonement, 76, 154
Augustine, 3, 129

Berdyaev, Nicholas, 160
Buddhism, 147

Caputo, John, 152, 154
causation, 11, 26
choice, 21, 44, 51, 54, 58-62, 82. *See also* freedom
coherence (of Kierkegaard's authorship), 113-15, 132, 145
Come, Arnold B., 150
communication, 66, 87-89, 115, 120-22, 148

Concept of Anxiety, The, 123-25, 131, 150
Concluding Unscientific Postscript, 18, 21, 52, 58, 129
Constantin Constantius, 67-88, 93, 98
continuity, 18-19, 75-76, 146
contradiction: Aristotelian, 14-15, 18, 49, 52, 82; Danish debates concerning, 41-45, 53; Hegelian, 15, 30-31, 49; Kierkegaardian, 15, 21, 34, 49-52, 54-55, 59-61, 65. *See also* difference
creation, 75, 77, 93
creativity, 138
Crites, Stephen, 152, 155
Cupitt, Don, 155, 158-59, 161

death, 107
Deleuze, 5, 17, 76, 83, 88, 132, 133, 138-39, 147
Derrida, 28, 107, 156, 157
difference, 65-66, 76, 81-82, 105-9, 114, 140, 146
Diogenes, 67-68, 93
double movement, 100, 106
doubt, 65-66, 94
dramatization, 33-35, 53, 68, 87-89, 122
dunamis. *See* potentiality; power
Dupre, Louis, 158

edification, 66, 87-88, 120-21
Edifying Discourses, 115-20

171

Either/Or, 37–39, 43, 49–66, 79, 83, 87, 113–14, 115, 119
Eriksen, Niels, 160, 161
eternal recurrence, 137–39
ethical existence, 38, 53, 58–60, 63, 74, 95, 113
ethics, 83, 92, 101, 156
Evans, C. Stephen, 159
existentialism, 3, 34, 96, 137–46

faith, 19, 77, 81, 86, 91–97, 99, 105–9, 114
fear, 104
Fear and Trembling, 2, 67, 81, 87, 91–110, 114, 115, 119
Ferreira, Jamie M., 158
fidelity, 86, 92, 105, 146
freedom, 16, 18, 21, 25, 27, 38, 51, 54, 55, 58, 60–61, 63–64, 73–74, 78, 82, 84, 95, 96, 100, 103–4, 107–8, 114, 145
Freud, 139
future, 58, 61–62, 71, 142

generality, 79, 83, 86, 104, 107, 156
gift, 78, 106–7, 114, 116, 142
God. *See* faith; transcendence; gift; grace; love
Goldschmidt, 37
grace, 77, 108, 158
grief, 57

happiness, 101–2, 106–10, 113, 159
Hegel, 1–3, 14–17, 21, 25, 27, 40, 72, 100, 150, 153; Kierkegaard's response to, 32–45, 50, 52, 57–59, 62, 73–74, 91–92, 94, 96, 100–1, 106, 119, 122–24, 127–33, 147; Hegelian logic, 27–28, 30–32; Hegelian theology, 29
Heiberg, J. L., 40, 73–74, 79, 87
Heidegger, 5, 17, 68, 107, 114, 128, 129, 137, 140–44, 150, 159
Heraclitus, 10, 14, 18, 56, 75, 93, 142
history, 97, 130, 140
Hobbes, 23–24
Hume, 26, 30

Husserl, 140, 162
Hyppolite, Jean, 28

idealism, 10–12, 51, 68, 71, 73, 82, 114
immanence, 28, 42, 45, 61–62, 71–75, 77, 130, 134, 156
immortality, 59
incarnation, 21, 29, 42, 86, 107, 123, 130
incommensurability. *See* difference
indifference. *See* nihilism
inwardness, 1, 2, 18, 21, 49–51, 60, 63, 66, 72, 78, 81, 83, 89, 92, 95, 100, 102–7, 113–14, 116–19, 122, 125, 128–29, 134, 138, 147
Isaac, 91, 99

James, Letter of, 116–117, 124
Jesus, 20, 21, 29, 72, 76, 117, 119
Job, 69, 85–88, 105
Johannes de silentio, 81, 91, 94–99, 105–6, 146
joy. *See* happiness
Judaism, 29, 42, 44
Judge William, 38–39, 51–53, 55, 57, 74
justice, 101

Kant, 23, 25–30, 101, 131–32
kinesis, 9, 15, 16, 18, 19, 22, 26, 40, 49, 52, 55, 59, 63, 66, 68, 72, 73, 78, 87, 89, 91, 95, 114, 122, 128, 145, 157
knowledge, 62–67, 71, 72, 83, 114, 117–19, 122–23, 145

language, 124
law. *See* generality
leap of faith, 20, 21, 62, 92, 100, 106–9, 157
Leibniz, 24, 75, 153
Lessing, 157
Levinas, 154, 156
love, 63–64, 81, 86–87, 92–93, 97, 99–100, 102–8, 114, 116–17, 119, 141, 145, 146, 158

Martensen, H. L., 34, 40–44, 49
mediation, 1, 5, 16, 30–32, 40, 42–45, 51, 54, 57, 59–60, 72, 74, 77, 88, 92, 94, 96, 106–7, 114, 124, 129–31

melancholy, 37, 56-57, 83-84
moment, 77
Mynster, Bishop, 41-45, 49, 51, 59-60

necessity, 61, 65, 73, 96, 101, 107
Nietzsche, 5, 21, 23, 109, 132, 133, 137-40, 143, 145, 146
nihilism, 54, 56-57, 82, 83, 118, 138, 144
non-realism, 108, 135, 158-59

ontology, 128

paganism, 20-21, 71-72
pantheism, 135
Paul, St., 118
paradox, 21, 98, 106-7, 130, 134
Parmenides, 10-11
passion, 19, 20, 56, 85-86, 92, 93, 95, 96, 99-102, 130, 134
patience, 117-18, 142-43
Pattison, George, 154, 161-62
Philosophical Fragments, 77, 107, 122-23, 157
philosophy, Kierkegaard's attitude to, 4, 37, 50, 53, 57-58, 68, 78, 80, 96, 121, 127-33
philosophy of religion, 146-47
plane of motion, 17, 23, 25, 30, 49, 66, 70, 128, 130, 145, 147
Plato, 10, 11, 70
Point of View for My Work as an Author, The, 88
potentiality, 12, 13, 15, 16, 23. *See also* power
power, 23-26, 55, 59, 74, 76, 85-86, 92, 93, 95, 103-4, 108-10, 114, 116-17, 128, 130, 134, 137, 146
practices, religious, 147
pseudonyms, Kierkegaard's, 121-22
Pyper, Hugh, 159

receptivity, 78, 106-9, 114, 116-17
recollection, 2, 57, 68, 70, 77, 78, 114, 122, 153

Regine Olsen, 15-16, 121
religious writing, Kierkegaard's. *See Edifying Discourses.*
Repetition, 2, 4, 24, 54, 67-89, 91-93, 95, 96, 98, 102, 114, 115, 119
repetition, 21, 51, 57, 68, 69, 93, 102, 114, 116, 118, 121, 125, 138-40, 146, 147
resignation, 81, 91, 93, 98, 100-6

Sartre, 144-46, 149, 150, 152
Schelling, 11, 35
secrecy, 50
selfhood, 120-21, 134, 137-38, 143
Sibbern, F.C., 41-42, 59
Sickness Unto Death, The, 125, 154
sin, 63-64, 123-25, 154
singularity, 79, 86, 104, 107, 156
skepticism, 28
Socrates, 70-71, 73, 122
soul. *See* inwardness
Spinoza, 14, 23-28, 109, 129, 133-35
Stack, George, 149
Stewart, Jon, 150
subjectivity. *See* inwardness; selfhood
substance, 13-15, 20, 24, 134
suffering, 85, 93, 99, 102-3

theater, 88
Tolstoy, 151-52
transcendence, 42, 44-45, 62, 73-75, 78, 79, 86, 105-8, 113, 116, 135, 158
Trendelenburg, 40, 122
truth, 50, 63, 66, 67, 70-73, 77, 78, 81, 82, 86-87, 89, 91-92, 95, 104-5, 116-20, 123, 129, 141-47

Walsh, Sylvia, 162
Weil, Simone, 158
Wittgenstein, 133, 146
women, 80

Printed in Great Britain
by Amazon